MW01633976

A BOY CALLED MAN

Passing the A.C.E Test

BY

GARY D. FALLINGS

ISBN:

978-1-963502-98-5 (Hardcover)

DEDICATION

This book is dedicated to my children. I want you to know that there is nothing that you are unable to achieve. Life is hard. No matter the circumstances - NEVER GIVE UP! Everything that I do is because of you! I love you!

To my mother, I could not have become who I am without you. Your faith, support, unconditional love, and resilience have motivated me to set goals and to be relentless in accomplishing those goals. You are the epitome of a "strong BLACK woman!" I thank you for all the time, love, and affection that you poured into me and my siblings. I love you!

To all the men who played a minor or major role in my life, thank you! I learned from the good, the bad, and the ugly! I dedicate this book to my father, stepfather, uncles, cousins, and all men dealing with trauma, mental illness, drug addiction, alcoholism, and incarceration.

To all the children that I have had the pleasure of teaching, coaching, mentoring and interacting with, please do NOT allow your current circumstances to control your future.

PRACTICE INTELLIGENCE OVER EMOTION! THINK!

YOU MAKE ME BETTER! YOU ARE VALUED!

Table of Contents

ACKNOWLEDGMENTS

I thank God!

I am grateful to the City of Harrisburg, Pennsylvania. We all know that growing up here is an everyday fight for survival. However, there are many great people who come from our city. Who will be next to achieve greatness?

I would like to say "Thank You" to Mrs. Mobley and the Harrisburg School District for providing an opportunity to help improve children's lives through **education**.

To my friends and family, I want to express my gratitude, love, and appreciation for you. Please know that you have molded me into the man that I have become from birth to the present. Your love and support keep me moving forward and striving for excellence. I represent you wherever I have been and wherever I go (**environment**). We are family!

I am indebted to Coach Chis and the Harrisburg Packers organization for modeling the **expectations** of a man. The "Borrowed Fathers" that spent countless hours away from their families in an effort to develop little boys into men. Thank you for **exposing** me to "manhood."

**EDUCATION+
ENVIRONMENT+EXPOSURE+EXPECTATIONS**

The order does not matter

PASSING THE A.C.E. TEST

"Feel the pain, feel the joy of Man that was never a Boy."

DMX

"According to the U.S. Centers for Disease Control and Prevention, approximately 60 percent of the population reports at least one ACE (Adverse Childhood Experience)." The CDC (Center for Disease Control and Prevention) emphasizes that "adverse childhood experiences can have a tremendous impact on future victimization and perpetration, and lifelong health and opportunity."

The Substance Abuse and Mental Health Services Administration (SAMHSA) has done extensive research on the effects of childhood trauma. "Research indicates that more than two-thirds of children reported at least one traumatic event by the age of 16 (SAMHSA, 2015). Experts have discovered that children who have had traumatic experiences are more likely to experience learning problems, more suspensions and expulsions, increased use of health and mental health services, increased involvement with juvenile justice and child welfare systems, as well as long-term chronic health problems (2015).

Throughout my life, I have worked with thousands of children. The relationships developed while teaching, mentoring, and coaching in the Harrisburg community have helped me understand my own life. I believe that many of us who are working with our children are "self-medicating."

As we learn more about the lives of our children and the adverse childhood experiences that affect our children, we somehow develop a better perspective of our own childhood. The trauma that we "overcame" begins to resurface as we attempt to help others cope with traumatic childhood experiences. If we take the time to self-reflect on our past, we become highly effective when working with youth dealing with adverse experiences in a healthy way. We are better able to make the connections, empathize, and provide supportive services that benefit our children.

I began working with children when I was just a young kid, 15 years old, to be specific. I was a sophomore in high school when the school district decided to create a class to develop young leaders. The class was called Peer Leadership. Peer Leadership was not available to all students, and most of the students were "hand-picked" by teachers. The class was held during lunch times, which meant that students would not be able to "double grub." "Double grubbing" was what Mr. Smith, the high school principal, referred to students who skipped class to attend both lunch times. Mr. Smith monitored lunch to deter students from hanging out during both lunch times. Ironically, the students enrolled in the Peer Leadership course chose to spend both lunch periods hanging out in the class.

Mrs. Mobley was the teacher of Peer Leadership. Mrs. Mobley was absolutely downright dope! She was tall, she stood about 5'9", she was high-yellow, she had a beautiful tan during the summer, she had curves (not to be disrespectful), she was intelligent, caring, sophisticated… she could out-dress the finest women on television. She was just beautiful! Mrs. Mobley had high expectations for her students and held us accountable for our actions or inactions. She did not take any "mess" from anyone! I respected her and valued the training, information, and tools she gave us to be influential young leaders.

The Peer Leadership class provided opportunities for students to see a different world. Mrs. Mobley planned educational trips that allowed the students to grow and gain new perspectives on life. For example, Mrs. Mobley arranged a weekend retreat for the Peer Leadership group in the Poconos, Pennsylvania. During the retreat, we received leadership training, conflict resolution training, entrepreneurship, and business development and participated in team-building activities. There were times when students became frustrated and argumentative. However, the group was encouraged to work together to find solutions to problems. I remember a very simple but difficult challenge that took multiple attempts to complete successfully. Eight students had to stand on a tree stump with a 20-inch diameter. Impossible! After some time, we discovered that we had to think "outside of the box." We accomplished the goal utilizing INTELLIGENCE over EMOTION. The more frustrated we grew, the more complex the task became. However, once we removed the emotion, we were able to clearly think and work together. This was a great experience. Many of the students may have never had a chance to visit the Poconos. However, Mrs. Mobley was intentional in providing meaningful experiences for the students.

I recall working with a troubled little girl whose family I had grown up in the same neighborhood. The young lady always seemed to be upset. She was quiet, light-skinned, had curly hair, and wore thick bifocals. She had a strange habit of staring at people. It was very awkward for me, and I was a pretty big guy. This young lady would stare as if she were looking through a person. One day, I caught her giving me the "evil eye," so I decided that this was my opportunity to build a positive relationship with her. I approached her, being my usual cool and silly self. She quickly withdrew and became irritated with me. I was persistent. I figured that maybe she "needed" my help but was being cautious with her feelings. They say persistence is the key to building trust… well, not this time. She gave me a fair warning!

"Leave me alone", she shouted. I continued to make jokes! She told me, "Get outta my face"! I continued laughing and joking. She said, "I am gonna hit you!" I jokingly said, "No, you will not; you better not hit me." She thought about it, grabbed her lunchbox, and BUSTED me in the head with her lunchbox! It was hilarious! I could not believe that a six-year-old kid had the nerve to hit me in the head. I did not get upset. In fact, I became more empathetic towards her family and her upbringing. I was close friends with several of her cousins, so close that we called each other "cousins." I knew she had it rough, but I had hoped that I could make her smile or laugh. She was taught to be cautious of all men, which led to her distrust of me. I learned that you must always give children their space and not intrude on their space. I understood that it would take time to gain her trust. Patience is key when working with our youth. That evening, I went over to hang out with her cousins. Her cousins and I laughed about the experience, but I never said a word to her about hitting me. In her mind, she was protecting herself from harm. I knew that deep down, she regretted hitting me, so I never reminded her about it.

I was a member of Peer Leadership until I graduated from high school. The following summer, I applied for a job at the Boys and Girls Club as a Cadet Camp Counselor. I had the best experience of my life working that summer. I was working with Coach Sherman Cunningham and his son, Daryl. Not to mention that I was working alongside one of my closest friends, Tarik. We had a wonderful time educating the youth while providing structured activities for the children. The field trips to the swimming pool, movies, skating, museums, zoos, and amusement parks were enjoyable. However, the overnight camping trips exposed the children to a totally different life.

Have you ever had to survive in the woods? Sleep outside in the open forest with only a tent and a sleeping bag? No cabin. No air mattress. Have you ever had to cook breakfast, lunch, and dinner on an open fire? What about using iodine to cleanse the spring water? How about going to the bathroom digging holes when you need to do the number 2? Hiking for miles, uphill, downhill, over the brush and fallen trees, through the small streams of cold water… this is what living in the wild is all about! Not to mention waking up to skunks, raccoons, and snakes in your tent.

We had an awesome outing outdoors every time! I must admit that I was a bit skeptical in the beginning. First, I had a girlfriend I did not want to be away from for several days. Secondly, I am from the city and like sleeping on a bed inside a house. Lastly, I liked eating junk food and cereal all day. My apprehensions had nothing to do with the children. I was worried about my comfort until a student asked me, "Mr. Gary, are you going?"

Without hesitation, I replied, "Yes, I am". One thing that I learned early in my career is that I am passionate about children. You have to lead by example. Therefore, it was imperative that I join the children on the camping trip. Our children are watching everything that we do and don't do. Modeling is essential to earning the trust of young men. There is an old saying, "Never ask someone to do something that you cannot or are not willing to do yourself!"

The camping trips were an opportunity to show and prove that we were capable of keeping the students safe. There were so many risk factors that could have led to a disaster. Supervision is key! Setting limitations is essential!

Imagine three big, black dudes, lookin' like the singing group "Full Force," being responsible for 25 boys and girls, ages 6-11, in the wilderness! We built great relationships with their mothers, grandmothers, and caregivers. We understood our roles as "men." We NEVER disrespected them or took advantage of our roles by crossing the line. Unfortunately, there were not many fathers coming around. We were the children's "fathers." We were their "uncles" and "big brothers." Black men have a huge responsibility to change the mindset of our children, especially young males. The challenge is to show children something different than what they have grown accustomed to in their short lives… exposure! The old saying, "You can't teach an old dog new tricks," or "Children learn what they are taught," means that we must be intentional in all interactions with the youth.

I believe that there are three components to helping a child overcome adverse experiences. The three most important factors that change students' lives are education, environment, and exposure! These three important things helped the main character in this story overcome the trauma. Mrs. Mobley, the Peer Leadership teacher, understood the value of these three things and provided us with a unique, rewarding, life-changing experience.

Post-traumatic stress disorder (PTSD) is uncommon in children. Studies show that 14% to 43% percent of young children are diagnosed with PTSD. However, what about those students who do not show signs of PTSD or simply do not talk about traumatic experiences in their lives? These children are too often neglected by the system that is responsible for protecting them. Just like adults, children sometimes keep secrets. Many children are taught to keep secrets so as not to embarrass the family or themselves. By revealing these secrets, they expose themselves to others who judge them, causing the child to be embarrassed or ashamed.

Man manipulated and deceived the system by exceeding the expectations at school. He understood the message from his mother, "What happens at home, stays at home!" There were consequences for "puttin' momma's business in the street." Man was able to prove that students from dysfunctional families and disadvantaged communities are capable of academic achievement. The school became a haven to escape the madness at home temporarily. There were situations that were too embarrassing to share with others. Throughout his life, he would utilize his anger and hatred towards his father and stepfather to be the best MAN he could be!

The school was not the only positive outlet for Man. He began playing football at six years of age. They say that "EVERYONE NEEDS A WIN!" Winning became a habit! This is the place that made him a MAN. For years, he had suffered at the hands of others; he had watched his mother and sisters be physically beaten, and he did nothing. The time was coming! Man developed the courage to confront any and all issues on the football field.

Man's childhood experiences will help millions of young men confront their troubled past and overcome the trauma that has held us back too long. The domestic violence, bullying, physical abuse, and mental abuse depicted in this story will reveal what it was like growing up in the hood for a young black man. The experiences of Man are the EXPERIENCES of MANY MEN! In a sense, he is EVERYMAN.

At some point in a man's life, in order to fully understand who he is and what he wants to be, he must confront the horrors of his past. It is an extremely difficult challenge to share the pain with outsiders because no man wants to reveal his weakness, his fears, and his tears. Man has stepped forward to disclose to the world the life of a black boy growing up and becoming a MAN.

Man was a brown skin, short, chubby, quiet kid. He had short hair, but he wore a "Shag." A shag was the style back then; the shag was a haircut that was even all around, except the back, along the neckline. The shag was a thick puff ball across the back of the neck. Man loved his Shag. As a matter of fact, he enjoyed going to Mr. Henderson's barber shop. Mr. Henderson was a big fellow with a deep voice. He was a well-dressed man, a gentleman, a God-fearing man. Man thought the world of Mr. Henderson; he was always so kind and caring, and he smelled good all the time. Man admired Mr. Henderson. Mr. Henderson prohibited his customers from cursing in front of children; everyone respected his wishes. Life was "good" at Mr. Henderson's barbershop. Man felt safe.

Safety and security are key to a child's physical, mental, social, and emotional growth. Along with education, safety and security are among the top responsibilities for schools to provide for students. Ivy Prep says, "When a child feels secure, they feel safe. This is not just a sense of physical safety, although that's extremely important. But it is also a feeling of emotional safety and security. Children need to feel that it is okay for them to express their emotions." Children build confidence in safe and secure environments. This confidence transcends in the classroom as students develop positive relationships with peers and adults at school.

"When I was five years old, I realized there was a road, and at the end, I would win lots of pots of gold! Never took a break, never made a mistake... took time to create cuz it's money to make." Kool G Rap

When he was five years old, Man began to realize that life takes you down many roads. He spent the majority of his life searching for the "pot of gold" on the "Road to the Riches." The streets and roads he traveled were never rich or affluent. Man's family lived on Zarker Street—a tiny little one-way street that hid behind the "Murderous" Market Street. On Zarker Street, Man's paternal family lived in four houses. His father's mother and two sisters lived side by side. The family was close and stuck together no matter the situation, which was not always a good thing! Man's most traumatic experiences occurred on Zarker Street, where the family lived, but there was no protection.

All of the action was on Market Street. Men and women hung out all day and night. There were three bars on one block. They were Fab's, Crow's, and Times. These were the bars where the pimps, drug dealers, and street folks gathered to have a good time. Mr. Henderson's Barber Shop was next door to Fab's. Many people lost their lives on Market Street. Man's favorite place was on Market Street, Green's Bakery. Every day, he would ask his mother for 50 cents to purchase the delicious, creamy peanut butter buns, the cinnamon packed between layers of rich, moist dough. The 5&10 and Superior Store catered to the Black community. The 5&10 sold Black hair products and cashed checks. Superior Stores would accept food stamps and sell the best meat. Market Street was a money-making area. The drug dealers and "winos" loitered the block day and night. The street was later changed to Martin Luther King Boulevard. Unfortunately, a great, influential African American leader's name is attached to many of the worst streets across the nation.

Despite the environment, Man's mother was determined to expose her children to a different life. Within 100 feet of their home, there was a private Catholic School, St. Francis. Although Man did not attend private school, his mother enrolled him and his siblings in the Head Start program and Summer program. The Head Start program was intended to give preschoolers an advantage upon entering school. At some point, the Head Start program was moved to the Berryhill Boys and Girls Club. The Boy's and Girl's Club fed the students breakfast when they arrived at the program. The meal program was important because students were provided with a healthy meal, which may not have been possible at home. The Berryhill Boys and Girls Club continues to provide effective programs and activities in the Harrisburg Community. For Man, the Berryhill Boys and Girls Club would always be a place of comfort.

At age 5, Man was lost in the streets of Harrisburg. He went to school on the first day of school and did not return to the bus stop. It was a bright, sunny day; the wind and the temperature were still hot. Kindergarten is supposed to be fun; however, most spoiled children who are attached to their parents struggle on the first day if they are absent. Have you ever witnessed children crying when being dropped off at school? Well, Man was one of those children. His mother held him tight as she introduced him to his new teacher. She held him as long as she could before leaving for work. His mother did her best to comfort him, hugging, kissing, and reassuring him that he would be fine. She gave Man specific instructions on how to get on the bus after school. The teacher was to ensure that he boarded the "right" bus.

The day went well for Man. Although he was a "thumbsucker," making friends was easy for him. He enjoyed being around the girls and was comfortable interacting with females. At home, he had two older sisters and a lot of female cousins. Naturally, he gravitated to women. He met a little girl, Amelia. She was kind and had a warm spirit. At the beginning of the day, she kissed Man on the cheek and told him not to cry. During lunch, he and Amelia sat next to each other. At the end of the day, Amelia smiled and said, "See you tomorrow!" Man was as excited as she was for the next day of school.

After school, Man did as he was told by his mother and teacher. Things seemed to be going well for Man. Riding the bus was cool. The children were yelling and screaming! Everyone was excited to share with others about their first day of school. The bus driver reminded everyone to stay seated as he stopped at various bus stops. Man saw a familiar place, the Berryhill Boy's and Girls Club. Man had been here many times, and there were groups of parents waiting for the bus. They were waiting for their children. His mother told him she would be waiting for him at the bus stop. Man was confident that someone would be there as he exited the bus. He looked around. There was no one there to meet him. Children were running to their parents to share the exciting events of their day, but Man had no one to run to or share his good news with! He had a good day! Man stood watching the parents and children leaving in different directions. He wanted to cry, but he held back his tears and slowly began to walk up the hill. Have you ever watched a movie where the character is lost and finds his way home? The movies where someone is on the verge of giving up but miraculously, at the last moment, find civilization. At five years old, imagine how Man felt traveling alone for blocks! This seemed to be a recurring theme throughout Man's life.

Man had no idea how he was going to make it home. Obviously, he would walk. However, he felt helpless. He had no choice but to try to make it alone. So, he walked and walked and walked. The scene at the top of the hill was much different from the Club neighborhood. There were cars cruising up and down the street, trash on the sidewalks and along the curbs, loud music coming from houses and cars, and there were people everywhere. They were smiling and laughing, hanging on the corner, sitting on the porches, and washing cars. The streets were busy! Little children were playing together, and women walked together, pushing baby strollers. Everyone appeared happy. Man took it all in as he nervously walked down 13th Street. He was taught never to talk to strangers, so he did as his mother told him. This would become his personality. Born a Gemini, he was naturally an introvert.

Already, he had a distrust of people. He spoke to no one. He was nervous, but there was no fear.

The distance from the Club to Market Street was approximately nine blocks. Man followed others as they were walking in the same direction. As he approached the corner, he stood with strangers as they waited for the light to signal "Walk." Most young children are taught to "Look both ways before crossing the street. There were times when he stood alone on the corner, applying the rules that his parents had instilled in him. Man was hesitant. A few times, he had to double-check before crossing the busy streets. He had recently been taught "how to ride a bike by his older cousin, Jerome. As he walked down 13th Street, he wished Jerome had been there to protect him. Nonetheless, the life lessons taught by his cousin were valuable. "Don't talk to strangers" and "Look both ways before crossing the street" were rules that should never be broken. He continued to walk down the 13th. He noticed that there were Spanish people everywhere. At that time, Man was not aware of the difference between Puerto Ricans, Mexicans, Cubans, and Dominicans. He only knew that the big building was called the Spanish-Speaking Center. At five years old, he was an excellent reader. Man was so small that everyone appeared to be giants. He kept telling himself not to cry, "Don't be afraid, don't be scared... just keep walking." After what seemed like hours, Man looked up and saw a familiar sight. It was the firehouse on 13th Street. The firehouse was on the corner behind Market Street. He had walked by the firehouse many times with his mother and sisters. Jerome had taken him down by the firehouse when he was teaching him to ride a bike. Man's eyes began to water, his chest heaved up and down, and he felt a burst of energy from within. As he ran up Zarker Street, tears were streaming down his cheeks. His mother was standing in the middle of the street. She had been worried about him. She noticed Man running towards her, with her arms spread wide, crying tears of joy. She ran towards Man. The entire family was there. His sisters, aunts, and cousins were all screaming and filled with relief that Man had safely returned home. They asked questions like: "Are you okay?" "Where were you?" "Did you ride the bus?" The questions poured in, but Man did not say a word. He hugged his mother tightly as she walked him into the house. Once things were settled, his mother blamed the teacher and the bus driver for Man getting off at the wrong stop. Man blamed no one but himself. Also, he was amazed at his ability to get home without any adult help. He felt like a Man.

Man does not recall his father being there when he got home. They said that he was out looking for Man. Man did not have many memories of his father. The things that he remembered, he wished that he could forget. Emanuel, his father, was a well-dressed, smooth guy with a decent build. He had the physique of a former athlete who spent his night drinking too much beer. Man was grateful for two things that his father had given him. At 2 or 3 years old, he had bought Man a motorized Police motorcycle. Man loved riding that motorcycle. He would cruise the sidewalks of Ivey Lane all day. The other gift was a Doberman Pincher, Midnight. Midnight was Man's dog. Midnight was a beautiful dog. Emanuel took good care of the dog. Midnight was vicious. No one could come close to Man without Midnight growling. Midnight responded to Emanuel only, so the dog had to be chained in the backyard most of the time. Emanuel was never home.

Nevertheless, Emanuel took great care of Midnight because he and the dog had the same personality. They were mean, and the dog took on the Emmanuel's personality. As Man grew older, Emanuel's personality would become a major influence on his life.

Emanuel and Janet were a beautiful brown couple. Janet, Man's mother, was tall and sophisticated. She had short hair that was always styled and neatly cut. She was 5'10, brown-skinned with big hips. She loved to get dressed up and wear high heels. She had style. They say she had a walk that would make men wreck their cars as they drove down the street. They were a popular couple. There were always people hanging in the backyard of Ivey Lane. People sat around "playing the dozens," telling stories while drinking and smoking. There was always a lot of booze and beer at the party. Oh, there was plenty of food, too! The family would host cookouts regularly, grown-ups partied, and the children enjoyed playing in the creek. Once the children were asleep, the party continued, mostly gambling. The grown-ups would play Blackjack, Spades, Jim Rummy, and Tonk until the early morning. Man enjoyed waking up early in the morning to pick up the quarters and change that had fallen during the night. Sometimes, the card games would continue until mid-morning. There was always someone who partied too hard, sleeping on the couch. These were the good times. They did not last long.

Man's memories of his childhood are clear. Nothing is fabricated. There are very few memories of good times. His life seemed to be filled with trauma... one traumatic experience after another. There are so many children who grow up in situations like Man's. This story is not unique. I am grateful that Man was willing to share his story with me and the world.

Too many children are suffering in this world without a voice. Man is their voice—the spokesperson for children throughout the world who are coping with adverse childhood experiences.

Emanuel and Janet loved to party. They were young, in their 20s, and the nightlife was too tempting to avoid. They lived within a block of the most happening street in the Burg. It was the late '70s. Blacks were just getting a taste of freedom. Martin Luther King and Malcolm X, along with many others, were instilling in Black people the idea of taking pride in themselves, being independent, and standing up for themselves. Since the house was close to the scene, Man's aunt often left their children with Man and his siblings. Aunt Trish, Janet's sister, had four children: three girls and one boy. The oldest was Kerry-Ann. She was in charge of watching all of the children. Next, there was Wayne, Leslie, and Shana. Aunt Shirley, Emanuel's sister, had three children... Danny, Jimmy and Johnny. Emanuel's sister, Linda, had one child, Jerome. Aunt Shirley and Aunt Linda's children rarely stayed overnight because they lived next door to Big Mama, Emanuel's mother.

One day, while Man's parents were out partying with his aunts, Midnight got loose. There were no adults around. They were still out from the previous night. Everyone was upstairs playing games and watching TV. Midnight began barking downstairs. It appeared he was running through the house. The children could hear the tapping of his feet as he dashed back and forth from upstairs to downstairs. Everyone panicked. Kerry-Ann ushered everyone into the middle room. Midnight came running upstairs. He was barking and growling at anyone who attempted to leave the room. The older children challenged each other to return Midnight to the backyard.

No one dared to open the door. At five years old, Man became frustrated. He was tired of being scared. He was fed up. After being held hostage by Midnight for what seemed like hours, Man decided to take action. The older children watched in amazement as Man opened the door slightly enough for him to slide out. The other remained in the room. Man told everyone that he was going to get him. "I'm going to get him," he said in a Manly voice. He slid out the door; Midnight was in the bathroom drinking water from the toilet. Man grabbed Midnight by the collar and pulled it out of the bathroom. Midnight had rummaged through the entire house, knocking things down, eating the trash, and destroying furniture. Man scolded Midnight as he dragged the dog down the steps. Midnight was much bigger than Man, but he whimpered as if he knew he was wrong. Man dragged him through the living room and kitchen before pushing Midnight out the back door to the yard. Everyone came running down the steps. They were relieved. No one could believe that Man had the courage to step up when others were too afraid. Man felt like a MAN. Man has never had another pet in his life.

Do you think he was traumatized by the event?

The cousins spent a lot of time together, mostly on the weekends. Parents have to be careful with who babysits their children. Often, parents are concerned about strangers who may harm their children in their absence. Unfortunately, children are frequently hurt by those they love. Sometimes, you have the "blind leading the blind." For example, Man tells a story of being forced to watch horror movies with his older cousins. Currently, he still hates watching scary movies. Trauma can come in various forms. We have to be careful with what we expose our children to in the development stages.

They were called "sleepovers." The children would arrive in their pajamas; snacks would be placed on the kitchen table, and everyone would huddle together until they fell asleep. Kerry-Ann and Wayne were the eldest, and their ages ranged from five to 14 years old. Kerry-Ann and Wayne loved to watch scary movies. It was the 70s, so black folks did not have colored televisions in every room. Some families did not own a TV at all. So, the kids would have to watch the same programs. Because Kerry-Ann and Wayne were the oldest, everyone was forced to watch scary movies late at night. *Salem's Lot* would have adults pissing in their pants and not being able to sleep at night. The movie was horrifying. Man was truly shaken, as were the others. No one dared to leave the room. The children were afraid to go to the bathroom. Those who had to go simply had to wait for someone else to have a tingle. They went to the bathroom in three's! Man has never forgotten that movie or that night. He resented his cousins for years because he was forced to watch the movie. Wayne said, "Be a man and stop being a punk." Man watched all he could and resented his cousin for it. Man avoided watching scary horror movies at night until he was in high school. He finally overcame the trauma.

Do you see how important it is to have responsible adults supervise your children in your absence?

Janet had a good job working for the State. She was a dedicated hard worker with only a high school education. Janet was raised by her father. He worked long hours at the steel mill, so Janet was left in the care of her older sister. Her mother passed away when she was seven years old. Janet was the youngest of four children. Trish was the eldest, followed by Pete and Carroll.

At this time, Pete and Carroll did not have any children. Trish was tough, she did not take shit from anyone. She worked for the State, too. She and Janet were often mistaken for one another because of their close resemblance. Pete was the only boy. His father was very protective because Pete was born with learning disabilities. Pete was not retarded. He simply functioned a little slower than others. There was no such thing as autism. Carroll was quiet. Although she looked like her sisters, she was short, heavy-set, and had a mole underneath her nose. Carroll was the smart one in the family. She had attended college in the South. Despite losing their mother early in life, all of the children had graduated from high school. They would ensure that their children did the same.

Janet was the money-maker in the Man's family. She worked two jobs most of her life to make sure that her children were fed and had a "roof over their heads." She was an amazing, strong woman and a great mother. She worked her butt off but made sure that the house was clean, meals were cooked, clothes were pressed, and bills were paid. Emanuel did not do much to help. He did not have a job. Maybe he did help. Perhaps he made enough money in the streets or gambling. Man had no idea what role Emanuel had in the house. Man only knew that Emanuel was a hell-raiser. Whenever he was home, there was fussing and fighting. He drank and partied all night, enjoying himself, but came home to inflict pain and misery on everyone else. Man hated him.

Man recalled the worst day of his childhood. Well, one of the worst days. There were so many. It was a beautiful day; the sun was shining, and it was hot. Man and his siblings were on the porch playing games. Janet was in the house preparing for the day. Emanuel had been out all night. When he returned home that morning, he smelled like alcohol. He did not acknowledge the children playing on the porch. He stormed into the house. Moments later, the children could hear their parents arguing. Emanuel's voice could be heard by the whole street. His mother, brother, and sisters came out to see what was happening. Emanuel had become physically violent and was dragging Janet up the steps to the second floor. Man and his sisters cried and begged Emanuel to stop. He ignored everyone. It was like he was possessed by an evil spirit. He continued his vicious attack on Janet while the children, his mother, and his sisters were helpless against the "monster." Emanuel beat her. He choked her. He raped her. You could hear the screaming, her cries, and pleas for help. No one came. Man and his sisters stood at the bedroom door, banging on the door, wailing, desperately waiting for someone to put an end to the senseless beating and rape. No one came. Man hated everyone that allowed it to happen. His uncle did nothing to stop the attack. He hated men for not intervening and protecting his mother, his sisters, and himself.

How can a man beat his wife and claim to love her? How can a man rape and torture the mother of his children? How could his mother, brother, and sisters approve of this? Man was devastated from that point. He lost love for people. Man was five years old, and his sisters were six and eight. How were they supposed to recover from this?

The experience was horrifying for the children. They had to watch their beautiful mother suffer at the hands of their father. He was a despicable animal, a savage beast. Man struggled to call him "Daddy." Man felt that Emanuel did not care about him. His father was a selfish man. He was destroying the family. He was on a rampage. Emanuel only cared about himself.

As Man shared his story, he began to address his father as if he were alive: "What type of man does this to his family? What would you do if someone were to beat your sisters that way? How could you commit those acts in front of your mother? Man had a second thought. What type of grandmother would allow her grandchildren to witness such a thing? Why did no one call the police?" Man had lots of questions, but unfortunately, those questions will never be answered. Despite not having answers, he continued to question his father. "What did she do to deserve that? Why was he so upset? Man referred to his father as "mean-spirited and evil." He told his now-deceased father that he would be the total opposite of him. Man vowed to protect his mother and sisters. He vowed to protect all women.

How does trauma affect young boys? How could this experience inspire Man to be better than his father?

Janet decided that she had enough. She no longer wanted her children to grow up in a violent home. Janet had a plan; she had to get out. She would stay with her father until she could find an apartment. One day, Emanuel was preparing to go out. As always, Emanuel would leave early and return late. Janet waited for Emanuel to leave. Immediately, she packed the children's clothes and called her cousin Alfred. Alfred was a former Marine who had earned two Purple Hearts. Alfred was different. He was laid back and smooth. He looked like money all the time. He was always dressed up like those "players" in the '70s. Alfred drove a big Fleetwood Cadillac with Whitewalls that he kept shining. Alfred would take Janet and the kids to his Uncle Dave's house. Uncle Dave (PopPop) had helped raise Alfred from childhood. Alfred's parents had died at an early age. Alfred and Janet grew up together and were raised by their parents' relatives. Alfred was considered to be Janet's big brother. He always came when she needed him to pick her up.

Soon, Janet found an apartment at Harrisburg Park Apartments on the other side of town. Now, she and the children had a home of their own. She was moving forward with her life. Emanuel would no longer be a part of their lives. She was at peace. She felt safe. It was not long before Emanuel found out where she was living. To her surprise, Emanuel showed up one night banging on the door. He was drunk as usual. The children were resting peacefully. They were awakened by Emanuel's hard knocks on the door. In the beginning, he pleaded to see his children. He was sweet and persuasive, but when Janet refused to allow him inside, he became furious. Emanuel broke the locks off the door. He rushed Janet, grabbing her and throwing her to the floor. Janet instructed the oldest of the children to call 9-1-1. He began pounding her with his fists! The children yelled for their father to stop. For some reason, he did. He was probably trying to leave before the police arrived. Nonetheless, he left. He would not return for quite some time.

The next time Emanuel showed up at the apartment was Christmas Day. It was late evening. Janet and the children had enjoyed Christmas. Janet always worked hard to provide for her children, but at Christmas time, she spoiled the children rotten. They had eaten dinner at Trish's house. When they reached home, Emanuel called, saying he had gifts for the children. Janet was hesitant, but she went against her better judgment. She felt bad for Emanuel and she felt terrible for her children. She wanted their father in their lives. All too well, Janet knew the pain of not having a parent in your life. Emanuel arrived a short time later, drunk. His hands were empty! There were no gifts! Janet had shared with the children that their father was bringing gifts for Christmas.

Janet was furious! She demanded that Emanuel show her the gifts. Then, he went into his pockets and pulled out two boxes of Cracker Jacks! Yes, you got it! The popcorn is in a box with a toy. There were three children. The eldest child was not biologically his child. However, she deserved a box of Cracker Jacks! Emanuel gave each of his children a "gift." Man was crushed. He had not seen his father in months! Again, he realized that his father did not care for him. Man hated him!

THE MARINE - A MAN'S MAN

Sly was a Marine and a "country boy" from Guyton, Georgia. He liked to wear jeans with a big belt buckle, cowboy boots, and "ten-gallon hats." Sly came from a big family. He had three older brothers, three older sisters, and a younger brother. His mother was a pistol-packing woman who raised her children to be tough. Sly's eldest brother, Jesse, was a National Champion wrestler for the University of Michigan. After Jesse had graduated from college, he allowed Sly to move in with him. All of the siblings would eventually move to Harrisburg. Sly was still in high school; he was not a good student, but he was very good at wrestling. After high school, Sly decided to join the United States Marine Corps. Sly thought he was tough; he was the only child to join the military. Sly had a love for guns. Believing he was a cowboy, being a wrestler, and joining the Marines, Sly possessed all the qualities of a "tough guy."

While in high school, Sly would spend his mornings looking out the window. Each day, he would wait for the tall, brown skin woman with the big hips to walk to the bus stop. He pretended that she was his girlfriend. He never approached her, but he prayed that one day, they would be together.

After spending his time in the Marines, Sly returned to Harrisburg. Sly was different now. He was a grown man. He had traveled the world with the Corps. Although he continued to wear his cowboy outfits, Sly had been exposed to the latest fashion while overseas. His confidence had grown while away. He remembered the woman that he dreamed about while out in the field. He was home and did all he could to find her.

In the meantime, Janet and Emanuel were still separated. Emanuel would continue to harass Janet anytime he saw her in public. Emanuel was a jealous and violent man. One day, Janet had gone out with her sisters and friends. They were hanging out at Fab's when Emanuel showed up. He had been drinking heavily. He was furious to see Janet out having fun. Emanuel attempted to mistreat Janet as he always had. However, Sly had been hanging out, too! He knew that Janet liked to party, so he would regularly go to Fab's. Sly observed Emanuel speaking disrespectfully to Janet and becoming aggressive. Sly, being a tough guy, intervened to protect Janet. Emanuel backed down. Sly and Janet would become a couple. Sly had won the heart of the woman he had been seeking for years.

Man was impressed when he met Sly. He felt Sly would stand up to his father and protect his mother. Man and his sisters no longer had to worry about Emanuel yelling and cursing, breaking down the doors, and hitting their mother. Emanuel never showed up again.

In the beginning, Sly appeared to be a good guy. After some time, he began to display the same behaviors that separated Janet and Emanuel. Sly did not like Man! Sly thought Man was getting in the way of his relationship with Janet. At five years old, Man sucked his thumb and slept with his mother every night. Sly thought that Man was going to be "gay," so he decided to "make a man" of the young boy.

Sly spent most of his time at his sister's house. His sister, Nette, had a good job, a big house, and four sons. Jerry, Nard, Stank, and Tootie. Jerry was the oldest, and Toot was the youngest. Sly loved his nephews. They were athletic, tough, and handsome. They were the complete opposite of Man. Man was short, chubby, shy, and quiet... a momma's boy! Man was two years younger than Tootie, so Man liked hanging out with Tootie (Toot). He considered Toot his protector, his big brother. Unfortunately, Sly had instructed his nephews to beat up Man as often as possible. Sly had decided that the best way to "toughen up" Man was to get him "beaten up." The nephews, not knowing any better, did exactly what they were told to do. Bullying was not a topic in those days. It was called "making you a man."

Why would Sly feel the need to make Man tough? Was Man shy, or had he experienced a traumatic event that resulted in him shutting down? How would this affect Man throughout his life?

GETTING BEAT DOWN

Although Man knew what he would encounter at Aunt Nette's house, he looked forward to visiting Tootie on the weekends. Together, Toot and Man would play with Man's toys. Man always had a lot of toys. Toot enjoyed visiting Man at Christmas time because Janet bought the best gifts. Aunt Nette treated her children well, too! Her house was the gathering spot for all of the neighborhood boys. Toot introduced Man to all of his friends, including RJ, TJ, and Michael. Man was younger than everyone, so they often took advantage of his innocence. Toot behaved differently when they were around. Toot was a jokester, so he enjoyed a good laugh. Too often, it was at Man's expense. Man was called "A gay guy," "sissy," "crybaby" and "faggot" by the older boys. Jerry, Nard, and Stank were on the wrestling team, so Man was used as a wrestling dummy. They would put Man in the "Spladle," spreading his legs, stretching his "nuts" until he shed tears. Man learned the "Crossface cradle" early because he was often placed in that position; it was Uncle Jesse's signature pinning combination in Michigan. His nephews performed the wrestling move on Man to perfect it. Sly would drink his beer and enjoy the assault. It was his way of punishing Man for being a "momma's boy." Janet was his woman; he had waited for years, and Man was interfering with his late-night lust. Man never told his mother a thing. He kept it to himself. He knew that Sly enjoyed it. Man hated Sly for setting him up every time they spent "quality time together."

Man was alone. There was no way that he could stand up to the older boys. He knew that he would lose the fight.

Everyone had a big brother. Man had no one. There was no one Man could call. There was no one to stand up for him. Toot had three older brothers. RJ had an older brother, Chad; TJ had an older brother, Michael, and all the other boys had a brother to "take up" for him. The bullying was extreme at times. Man would be the "neighborhood punching bag" for years to come. The abuse would not only physically make him tough, but mentally he would become unbreakable.

Wayne, his Aunt Trish's son, was the same age as Nard and Jerry. As a matter of fact, Wayne was just as smooth, athletic, and tough as any of the guys hanging on the porch. Wayne lived in Uptown. He had more clothes and sneakers than everyone. He was the only boy, his father's legacy. His father did not live with him, but he took great care of Wayne and his sisters. Wayne was different; he could do back flips and stand on one hand, and he loved to dance. Wayne had a weird sense of humor. He seemed to think that everything was funny. For example, while everyone else was frightened by Salem's Lot, he laughed the entire movie. Wayne was crazy. He loved to fight. Wayne was short and stocky but quick and strong. He walked and talked like a thug. Man always thought that Wayne would beat up the bullies in the neighborhood, but that never happened. Man never told Wayne what was happening. He knew that Wayne would get pleasure from it. He would only laugh at Man.

At times, Wayne would take advantage of the little thumb sucker. Man reminisced of the time when Wayne punched him in the face. He was six years old at the time, and Wayne was 13 years old. It was the weekend Trish had moved her family to Penn Street. Janet and Trish had gone out to party. Kerry-Ann and Wayne were left to watch the younger children.

Although Man hated the abuse, he wanted to be accepted by the older boys. There is a term for it, Stockholm Syndrome. This occurs when the victim feels connected to his abusers. Man was addicted to the abuse. Often, victims of abuse keep quiet and continue to allow the abuser to control them mentally and physically. Man thought the older boys were the coolest guys in town. He had no other friends to hang out with. All of the cool guys hung out at Aunt Nette's house. The guys would hang out on the porch until late at night. During the day, they would play basketball and baseball at Lincoln playground. Man would tag along, but because he was not athletic, he would stand on the sidelines and watch the others play. He learned early to stay out of the basketball games. Have you ever heard of "Booty"? Well, Booty was a basketball game that resulted in the losers being hit on the butt with the basketball. If you really wanted to hurt someone, you stand at half-court and "drill 'em" in the back. Man, being the smallest and worst player, felt that sting of the ball every time he played. He realized that it was best for him to watch from the sidelines. Man never liked basketball. Sly never bothered to teach Man how to play sports. Sly enjoyed watching Man lose. Man HATED Sly.

As Man thought of the hate that he had for Sly, he realized that all of the children in his family disliked Sly. Sly was not a nice person. He was mean and controlling. Man remembered a time when his cousins had stayed for a sleepover. Derrick lived down south in North Carolina. His mother would send him up north to spend the summer with Janet and her children. Shana was Aunt Pat's youngest child. The morning after the sleepover, Sly woke up in a piss-poor mood. As always, he intended to make everyone else feel his misery. He began the morning yelling and screaming at the children. Janet was not home. She had gone to work. Sly was in charge. As a former Marine, he continued to follow the routine of waking up and "cleaning up the bunk." However, he was past the point of cleaning himself. He now had children to do it for him. He was now the drill instructor. He began drilling out instructions to the children, but Derrick and Shana did not live there. They were offended by Sly's yelling, screaming, and demanding that they take part in the daily routine. They flat-out refused to clean. Sly thought he would handle the situation as he always did by responding with violence.

Derrick and Shana would have none of that. Derrick mentioned his father to Sly, gathered his belongings, and headed to his father's house. Shana did the same, but she walked three blocks down the street to Aunt Carroll's apartment. At this time, Aunt Carroll lived alone with her baby boy, Shane. Sly was pissed off! Man wished that he could have done the same. Although he hated Emanuel too, he hoped that Emanuel would come to rescue him. He wished he could run to Emanuel.

In 1980, The Harrisburg Packers, led by Coach Charles Chisolm, formed the Pee-Wee, Pony, and Midget football teams. The Packers were registering players for the upcoming season. Toot and his brothers were going out for the team. Man was only six years old but soon to be seven. He wanted to be like them, so he begged Janet to allow him to join the team. Janet had many concerns but trusted that Toot and the others would take good care of Man. Janet said, "Yes!" Man was nervous but excited to be one of the guys. All of the neighborhood boys were going out for the team. The girls in the neighborhood were joining the cheerleading squad. Man was happy that he was going to be a football player. In a strange way, he hoped that Sly would be happy too! Football was a "man's" sport!

Man was scared on the days leading up to the first practice. He had no idea what was going to happen when he got there. The little boy had never run for more than a block. He had no clue what position he wanted to play. He had never been part of a team. On the playground, he was never chosen to participate in the games with the older boys. Man knew that he needed help. He wanted to be ready on the first day. Again, he had no older brothers or anyone to turn to, so Man approached Sly to help him prepare for the first day. Reluctantly, Sly agreed to teach Man how to catch a football. Man was excited to learn how to catch, but he was happier that Sly had agreed to spend some time with him. Unfortunately, Man would regret asking Sly to help. Sly must have been in a bad mood. He appeared irritated by spending time with his "son." Man realized that day that he actually HATED Sly. Sly was being a dickhead, intentionally. Sly took Man to "Carnation Street Alley." He stood in the middle of the alley and instructed Man to stay at the other end. The problem was that Man was standing at the entrance of the alley, where cars were constantly turning onto Carnation Street, which was intersected by 17th Street. 17th Street was one of the busiest streets in the city. Carnation was a hotspot for drug dealing and gambling.

Nevertheless, Sly puts Man at risk by having him stand at the street entrance to catch a football. To make matters worse, Sly purposely threw the ball over Man's head so he could not catch it. Man realized that he had made a huge mistake, but he kept trying, knowing that Sly was sabotaging their time together. The feelings of excitement quickly changed. His feelings for Sly intensified. He HATED Sly. As Sly intentionally tried to break the boy down, Man knew one day that he was going to get his payback. Sly threw the football at Man's face numerous times, "drilling" the ball at Man, but Man never cried; he never let on that he was angry. After a few tosses back and forth, but mostly Man scrambling to get the ball before it rolled onto 17th Street, Man relieved Sly of the pain of helping him.

Zaki came unknowingly to save the day. Man and Zaki would pass the football back and forth until nightfall. Man returned home that night, still burning inside with hate, but he was confused, too. He could not understand why he was treated so badly by his stepfather. A part of him thought that maybe his stepfather could not throw a football. He had been a wrestler from the South, so he COULD perhaps NOT THROW! No, that was not it. Deep down, Man knew that his stepfather truly did not like him. Man would never ask for his help again. Man was motivated to become a better man than Sly.

Football changed Man in so many ways. Some would say that football brought him "out of his shell." He had never played organized sports in his life. He had never done anything physical. He was a "momma's boy." The game of football seemed to make his mother love him more. He was good. He was a quick learner. And surprisingly, he was not scared. Once he put that uniform on, he felt like a warrior. He knew that the older boys would get preference, plus they all seemed to know each other. They were the same age and went to the same schools. Man was two years younger and attended Ben Franklin School. The school requires male students to wear a shirt and tie daily to school. The only way for Man to get noticed and get respect from others was on the football field. He had to go harder than the others. Toot had introduced Man to everyone as his "little cousin," but Man wanted to prove that he did not need Tootie to protect him. Well, Man got what he wanted sooner than he expected. Following warm-up and stretching, players were separated by position. Man had no idea what position he wanted to play. He just wanted to prove himself and be part of the team.

BOOM

BOOM!

He did it!

BOOM!

Man made the starting lineup.

BOOM!

Man was starting offense and defense. Man had found something to love, something to make him feel good about himself. This is key for anyone. Everyone has to find something they enjoy doing that fulfills their life. Everyone has a purpose. Some have more than one calling. Man had a purpose, and he found his calling.

The battle for a starting position was not easy for Man. He often found himself shedding tears on the football field more frequently than he would have liked. Despite his efforts, he struggled to control his emotions when the older boys upset or bullied him. Many people cry in such situations because they are hurting; they want to quit or feel they cannot win. Typically, the person crying will be embarrassed by the tears and their inability to hold those tears back. It was quite different for Man. His tears made him stronger, meaner, and more determined to conquer whatever was in his way. Each time he witnessed his mother being beaten by Emanuel and Sly, tears would fall on his cheeks. Every time he looked into his mother's eyes, he saw nothing but pain. Those tears represented the anger inside him, an anger that would one day be unleashed with the force of a tsunami—relentless, unyielding, and unstoppable. Those tears were his strength.

BOOM!

The PeeWee Packers had a great team. The competition was tough. The boys were two years older than Man. Fortunately, Man's cousin Trey was on the team, too! He was 11 days older than Man. John "JayJay" Lee was Man's brother from another mother who also joined the team as a first-year player. Man's best friend, James "Spitzy" Johnson, was the starting tight end. Herman Chambers was a relentless defensive end. Corey Matthews and Kevin Jackson were from Man's neighborhood. Corey and Kevin, the youngest players on the team and best friends, were often referred to as the "pretty boys" and played as running backs.

Both celebrated their birthdays in September, making Man three months older than them. In that first year, Man had the privilege of playing alongside a great group of guys, including Karl Singleton, Eddie Cowan, Ronald Stanton, Tyrone Richardson, Dwight Henry, Kevin Butts, Marvin Redcross, Zeffie Penn, Brian Brown, Orlando Putman, and Anthony McQuay. We won the Super Bowl the first year! We had great coaches like Sherman Cunningham, Vernon Lipscomb, Coach Perry Landon, Coach Henry, Coach Skip House, and Coach Nate McWhite, better known as Coach Mack. Practice was always fun.

The coaches appeared to enjoy being with the players. Man had never experienced this before. No man in his family was taking the time out of their day to spend time with Man. Man felt good about his relationship with the coaches. He wanted to be around them too. It was not just playing football that was changing Man, but he was seeing what a "good' man should be, how he should act, walk, and talk. The coaching was good, but these men specialized in building boys up and instilling high morals and values in young boys. They had high expectations for the players on the football field. However, they constantly preached about being good students, as well as being good people. They modeled the behaviors that they expected from the players.

Coach Sherm was that guy for all of the boys. He was the uncle of Corey Matthews. Coach Sherm had been an excellent high school football player and an all-around athlete. He had a deep, raspy voice that had so much energy in it that the boys were motivated simply by the sound of it. Coach Sherm was dark-skinned, cocky, and bow-legged. He was in great shape. He was a soldier in the Vietnam War. While at war, Coach Sherm had been stabbed, shot, and severely injured and lived to talk about it. Little boys admired and were awed at the scars and wounds on his skin from the war. Coach Sherm often amazed the players with karate kicks and kung-fu moves he learned in martial arts. He was *bad to the bone*!

The head coach was Coach Perry Landon. Coach Landon was different. He was light-skinned, spoke excellent English, and appeared more educated than the other coaches. Nonetheless, he was equally knowledgeable and twice as mean. Coach Perry did not tolerate disrespect from his players. At the drop of a dime, Coach Perry would tell the boys, "Take a lap" or "Take a couple of laps until you're ready to play football." Coach Landon was a family man. His son and daughter would be with him when he came to practice. Lil Perry was too young to play for years, but when he came of age, he was a force on the football field. His daughter was a pretty little chocolate girl named Yana. Yana was a cheerleader for the Pee-wee Packers. Coach Landon was very protective of his baby girl. Many may have wanted to, but no one crossed that line to piss off Coach Landon. No one!

Coach Henry was the father of Dwight Henry. Dwight's nickname was "Weedie". It was obvious that Coach Henry and his son had an exceptional relationship. Joy was expressed on the face of Coach Henry when watching his son learn the game of football. Coach Henry seemed to be a simple man. He did not dress fancy. He was not a big guy or a loud guy. Coach Henry was the type of guy who wore a button-up shirt, khakis, and sneakers to practice. Something stuck out about Coach Henry: the way he wore his hat. He always wore a baseball cap. The hat would lay on top of his head, but it was never pulled down over his forehead. It was as if he just threw it on. The brim of the hat was slightly tilted to the side. This made Coach Henry look like an old drunk hanging in "Wine Alley." They say that "Looks can be deceiving" Coach Henry worked his ass off to send his son to one of the best schools in the state.

How about Coach Skip House? Orlando Putman's father, the Mason, The Shriner, The Greatest! Coach Skip was a nice guy. He was empathetic towards the players. He understood that the boys were emotionally weak, and he focused on building and strengthening the mental and emotional well-being of the players. His son, Orlando, aka "Putman," was on the offensive line and was a defensive linebacker. Putman was a short, fat kid with slanted eyes like an Asian person. He had chubby cheeks like Gary Coleman. Coach Skip loved his son, and it showed. He never missed practice or a game. He invested in the best equipment to prevent his son from injuries. Man never heard Coach Skip yell at his son, and he definitely never mistreated Putman. Putman had a great father. Man only wished he had the same thing.

And then there was Coach Mack, the meanest, most brutal, most violent of all the coaches. Man loved and admired Coach Mack for so many different reasons. Coach Mack referred to players as "knuckleheads" and "brain dead." He was awesome, a "Man's man," and the perfect combination of a caveman and a gentleman! He became a gentle giant in the presence of his wife and daughter. The brute seemed to lose all his strength. He became powerless when his family was around. He had a great smile that he was unable to hold back. He clearly loved his family. His son, Phil, was older than Man. Phil played with the older boys. He did not resemble his father in looks, but he had the courage of a lion. Everyone loved Phil. He was cool, had a great personality, and was incredibly intelligent. Tragically, Phil lost his life in a boating accident shortly after graduating from college. Coach Mack never recovered from losing his only son. In Man's eyes, Coach Mack was hurting deeply inside. Man wished he could make it all better and take the pain away. Coach Mack, Ms. Barb (wife), and Stephanie (daughter) did not deserve to lose their "boy" in that way.

R.I.P. to Coach Vernon Lipscomb, who served as the equipment manager for the Packer football team. Unfortunately, his time with the team was short-lived, as he passed away early in the football season. Coach Lipscomb's presence and contributions are deeply missed. Coach Lipscomb had to be the coolest guy in the world. He had a mean stroll, wore these thick glasses, and spoke like he was an old pimp from the 1970s. His words came out slow and smooth. He never raised his voice or appeared upset.

Everything about Coach Lipscomb was fantastic. We lost a great guy early.

Rest in Peace to all of my heroes - The Harrisburg Packers Family!

"ANOTHER ONE BITES THE DUST"

In 1980, Queen released the song *"Another One Bites the Dust."* They say that every superhero needs a theme song, and for the Pee Wee Packers, this track became their anthem. Pounding their pads in rhythm with the song, the players intimidated their opponents as they approached game time. Before the game, all players had to be officially weighed in. The Pee Wee was structured. They lined up numerically before walking to the weigh-in station. You could hear them before you could see them! Pads pounding and chanting together… Boom, boom, boom! "Another one bites the dust!" Parents played Queen's song loudly from their cars, and the game day announcers played it at all home games. The song motivated the players. It became the theme song for the Harrisburg Packers. The Pee Wee Packers won the Super Bowl in 1980.

Let's take a second to look closely at the circumstances that year. More than 83% of the boys on the team were growing up without a father. Some studies show that there has been a significant increase in the number of black men in jail since 1980. In 1980, there were approximately 2.3 million prisoners in jail. The US Department of Justice states, "Between 1974 and 2001, the rise in first incarceration rates had the largest effects on younger age groups. The percent of persons ever incarcerated tripled among persons ages 25-29 and more than doubled among persons 30-34 and persons ages 35-39." It is a prime time for a young man who wants to settle down and raise a family. The incarceration rates continue to grow, and more families are left without a strong black male to teach them, protect them, and support them. It was a pattern that developed over 40 years ago! The problem is that black men continue to "play" victim to the system. In 1980, there were 143,000 black men in jail. In 2022, there were approximately 760,000 black men locked up. The Prison Policy Initiative reveals that there are "1,556 state prisons, 102 federal prisons, 2,850 local jails, 1,510 juvenile correctional facilities, 186 immigration detention centers… military prisons" and more.

Also, there are "half-way" houses, psychiatric hospitals, and shelters that are utilized to lock men away without providing effective treatment for emotional, mental, and social disabilities. Mental health is a severe problem in the black community. Man suffered like others. However, he was able to "fake it till make it," fooling all of the so-called professionals. On second thought, maybe he did not fool them. Perhaps they did not care. Was he fooling them or himself?

His mentality was developed on the football field, but there was much more involved than just going to practice. Man had to prove to himself that he could be one of the best on the field. So, the practice was enjoyable on most days. The coaches would say that school and football were the players' jobs. Man took pleasure in going to work. Preparation was the key to being successful on the field. At night, before he went to bed, he dedicated himself to doing three sets of 10 pushups. Man would spend lots of time standing in front of the mirror, shadowboxing. He imagined that someone was standing in front of him. At times, he imagined that it was Sly or one of the neighborhood bullies. He was always thinking of ways to become bigger and stronger than the neighborhood boys who were constantly "picking on" him.

Man has always had a strong belief in God. Despite all that was going on in her life, Janet remained steadfast in her commitment to God and made sure that her children were grateful for God's blessing. Man was a "momma's boy." Remember that he slept with his mother until Sly appeared in her life.

Many people have claimed to have seen an angel. Well, Man is one of the few people that claim to have witnessed the divine. As a seven-year-old boy, Man lies in his bed, sleeping. When he awakened, he recalled seeing an angel come from the light in his ceiling. He closed his eyes, and when he opened his eyes, he saw an angel. She was moving. Again, he closed his eyes, but the image did not disappear. Man was frightened. He ran to his mother's bed to sleep with her. "Ma, I saw an angel!" She responded, "Aww baby, did you?" Man was serious, "Ma, an angel came out of my ceiling."

Man stands on this 100%!

IT'S GETTING HOT IN HERE

This may seem far-fetched, but imagine yourself locked in a room for hours. The heat is over 100 degrees, and your throat is so dry that it hurts to swallow. You grow weaker by the minute. Now, imagine yourself in a room full of steam, the air so foggy that you can't see your hands in front of your face, let alone another person. You lie on the floor, gasping for air, taking short breaths from the cracks under the doors. This is torture, right? From the description, you might think of someone placed in a a huge burning furnace. Now, imagine a poor migrant crowded in the back of a semi-truck with 200 others, trying to reach the Land of Opportunity and Home of the Brave.

Well, maybe that is extreme. However, for a seven-year-old boy to be placed in a small room with excessive heat for hours or placed in a hot, steamy room with air seemed like torture. America has always been obsessed with controlling how others should look, how people should act, how people should dress… the size of individuals… men, women, and children. Obesity has always been a hot topic for medical professionals and school officials. Little children are often labeled as obese because the obesity index or BMI indicates that they are overweight. In "*30 Thoughts on Why the Surge in Obesity*," Lane Kenworthy reveals that "after holding constant at about 15% in the 1960s and 1970s, the adult obesity rate shot up beginning in the 1980s, reaching 35% in the mid-2000s."

Where am I going with this? Remember that Man was a chubby kid. According to the neighborhood guys, he was fat and gay. Now, he has completed his first year of football. He was told that he was too heavy to play Pee Wee football. He was only seven years old. He had two more years of eligibility to play on the Pee Wee level. If Man wanted to continue playing with his peers, he would have to lose weight. At practice, Man would wear a black garbage bag underneath his uniform to shed the pounds. The reason for the garbage bag was it served as a sauna suit for Man because his family could not afford a "real" one. Nonetheless, Man proudly put that trash bag on. He noticed his muscles were developing, and it felt good to be strong.

The YMCA on 6th Street had a sauna and a steam room in the basement. For a small membership fee, visitors were able to utilize the fitness facilities for an entire day. Man was not alone in being overweight. Cuzzin Trey was considered to be a little heavy, too. Despite the circumstances, this is where Man and Trey developed a bond that would last a lifetime. The two boys would play alongside each other from Pee Wee football to high school and then to college.

Sundays were reserved for the Midget League football games. This meant that Man and Trey had to be below weight before weigh-ins at 8 am. So, the boys would get dropped off at the YMCA every Saturday morning. They were given instructions not to leave the sauna or the steam room until their fathers returned for them. Sometimes, the adults took hours to return for the boys. It was torture sitting in the sauna, not being able to breathe, fearing opening the door because both fathers were quick to "get the belt." The boys would take turns lying on the floor. There was a small gap between the door and the threshold that allowed a small amount of air to help with the suffocation. It just did not seem fair to the boys; they complained and whined, but neither boy cried. They loved playing football. Their father loved that they were football players. So, the boys endured the torture, and they began to look forward to going to the YMCA on Saturday mornings. As the years went on, they wore trash bags and sauna suits while suffering from the heat and steam. Often, the sauna felt as if it were melting the plastic clothing. Nevertheless, Man and Trey were never overweight on Sunday. Man and Trey were captains of the football team.

What are the advantages of involving youth in sports at an early age? How does playing sports help victims of trauma overcome adverse experiences?

There has been extensive research on the advantages of participating in sports for children experiencing trauma before the age of 18 years old.

GOTTA FEEL THE FIRE

"Gotta Feel the Fire" is the title of this chapter, chosen to reflect the series of traumatic events in Man's life that were all centered around the fire. Sometimes, it was not the external fires but the internal fires that mentally damaged Man.

Despite having great success on the football field, life at home was heating up. Because Sly was not working full-time, Janet was working two jobs. Emanuel was not doing his part to take care of the children. Life was hard for Janet, but she was making it work. Janet had worked hard to improve her credit so she could purchase a home. She found a house less than a block away on Walnut Street. The family could relocate without the children having to change schools or make new friends in the neighborhood.

In the beginning, life was good on Walnut Street. The couple had purchased new furniture and a new Volkswagon van. Man had his own room, and Chante and Kieva shared a room. There was a third floor, but the children were too young to be out of sight. The house had a nice-sized yard parallel to a walkway behind Goodwill. The walkway went from Walnut Street directly to the playground in the back of Lincoln Elementary School.

Janet and Sly held family gatherings all the time. Both families enjoyed cooking in the backyard, drinking liquor, and playing cards. There seemed to be a lot of good times on Walnut Street. However, because of the trauma connected to that house, Man could only remember the life-changing events that forced him to become a MAN while still a BOY!

The previous year, Janet had purchased Man a nice winter coat. It was her pet peeve that she purchased the children new coats every year at Christmas. However, winter was coming quickly, and Man needed a new coat. Man had been out playing with his friends the year before in the rain. He had seen his mother dry wet clothes by the space heater. So, after coming in from the rain, he had a brilliant idea. He would place his coat on the space heater to dry from the weather conditions. How many people remember the puffy jacket? Everybody wore shiny waist-length winter coats. Unfortunately, the coat was fake leather. The space heater quickly burned a huge hole in the jacket. Man would be without a coat for the upcoming winter. As he shared his story, Man remembered peeling plastic from the heater. Hey kids, make sure your coat is real leather before using a heater or oven to dry it!

Man needed a new coat. Janet was unable to afford a coat at that time. One day, Janet came to Man to tell him that he was staying home from school. It was a secret. He was not to tell anyone that he did not go to school. Mysteriously, a gentleman picked Man up around school time. He introduced himself as James. He said that he was Man's godfather. This was strange for Man because he knew his godfather was Roy. James said he was taking Man shopping for new clothes and a new coat. Just like any eight-year-old boy, Man was happy to know that a man was spending some time with him. James was sharp! He dressed well and drove a big Lincoln Continental. James smelled like money, like a man with a nice job. James took Man shopping and out to eat that day. Man wondered who the stranger was to him. Man would not see or hear from James until ten years later.

The Pee Wee Packers had won the Super Bowl for the second year in a row. Janet was a Packer Mom. She worked the concession stands, helped pass out uniforms, and was fully engaged in the Packer organization. She hosted the Super Bowl party at the new house on Walnut Street. The entire team came to the party. Everyone was playing in the yard or dancing in the living room. The older players stood in the walkway doing their own thing. It was a great time for the boys, but the grownups enjoyed themselves, too!

Many parties occurred on Walnut Street. Janet was great at organizing, decorating, and hosting parties. Summer was when most of the parties took place. That summer, Janet was having a cookout in the backyard. Everyone from Sly's family was there. Uncle Alfred had just bought a new motorcycle. He was taking everyone on a ride. Man was next up to go for a quick spin. Uncle Alfred warned Man, "Keep your legs out. That pipe is really hot." Man was doing fine until the end of the ride. Man carelessly forgot about the hot pipe, and his calf touched the pipe as he dismounted from the bike! The skin from his leg smelled like bacon as it burned on the metal pipe. He was in extreme pain as he tried not to cry because the older boys were laughing at him. Uncle Alfred seemed to be amused by it, too. He joked, "I told you that it was hot," and chuckled with the others. The physical pain of the burn bothered him, but the laughing lit a fuse in Man. As an adult, the scar from the motorcycle ride can still be seen on the back of Man's calf.

The anger in Man intensified as the older boys began to take more advantage of his size and ignorance. Man was naive. He wanted to be accepted by the older guys. He had no brothers, so he enjoyed being with the fellas despite being ridiculed and bullied by them. They were all fans of the Worldwide Wrestling Federation, aka the WWF. During sleepovers, they would wake up early together to watch wrestling on television. At times, they would pretend to be some of the superstars. On Man's 8th birthday, the neighborhood was having a great time in front of his house. RJ, who had always been a comedian, asked Man to come close to him.

As Man responded to his request, RJ grabbed Man and put him in the "Power Driver." They were standing on the cement. RJ did the unthinkable. He executed the move. Man's head and neck were driven into the ground. Everyone was laughing. Man was furious. He knew that he could not beat up RJ, so he did nothing in return. RJ had a big brother, too. Moments later, TJ grabbed Man. He put Man in the "Power Driver." Again, Man's head was driven into the concrete. It was hilarious to all the boys. No one had his back. No one would take up for him. Man wanted revenge. The fire in Man was starting to burn. The fuse had been lit. However, Man did nothing. He hated that everyone was bullying him, but he was too afraid of the outcome to retaliate.

Man was beginning to feel that everyone was taking advantage of him. He no longer wanted to hang out with Toot and his friends. He always thought that Toot would defend him, but Toot was too busy laughing with the others to see how much mental and physical pain Man was dealing with from the abuse. Man decided that he would hang out with JayJay. He and JayJay were the same age and the same size, played on the same team, and enjoyed doing the same things! JayJay was an only child whose mother and father spoiled him with everything. His grandfather worshiped him! His aunts and uncles treated him like their own. JayJay and Man would sit for hours playing games, watching TV, riding bikes, or hanging on the porch watching people and cars on the street. They became best friends. JayJay was shortened to Jay. The two boys became inseparable. They had so much in common, yet they were very different. Jay was an extrovert, and Man was an introvert.

Man's moves were intentional. He realized at an early age that he did not have to subject himself to unwanted physical and emotional abuse. He had blamed his mother many times for holding on to men who constantly mistreated her and the children. Although he worshiped his mother, he could not help but think that she was unnecessarily placing her children at risk. Janet was a good woman. She had grown up with an overprotective father who kept a close eye on his youngest daughter. She was a beautiful young lady who did well in school. After graduating from high school, she gained employment with the State. While working at the State office, she was able to save her modest earnings to purchase the house on Walnut Street. Janet was good at "making a way when there was no way." Although she did not have a driver's license, she was able to save and improve her credit to purchase a van, too. Man was not fond of the van, a Volkswagon van. It was blue with a carpeted interior. Thankfully, Sly had installed a great audio system. The speakers were installed throughout the entire vehicle. The neighborhood children loved being driven to the Boys and Girls Club and Packer football games. The van was a family vehicle used to transport Janet to work and the children to school and activities. The only problem was that Sly was the only driver. Even worse, Sly rarely worked a full-time job, which meant that he had plenty of time to "run the streets."

Sly thought that he was a ladies' man. Despite being involved in a relationship, Sly often stayed out until the wee hours, drinking at one of the taverns on 14th Street. There were so many bars (Fab's, Crow's, Times, O.D's, and many more) on one block that the street became known as "Wino Alley." As a kid, Man would see men lying on the sidewalk by the 14th Street playground. They were often called "winos"—people who drank cheap wines like Maddog 50/50, Boones Farm, and Thunderbird. For less than $5.00, you could get absolutely drunk. For a guy without a job, that was just what he needed.

The problem was not that Sly drank alcohol, but too often, his personality would change for the worse. He would go from a somewhat quiet guy to a loud, belligerent, tough guy who thought every woman would drop to her knees to be with him. He felt that he was "God's gift to women." Ironically, he spent all of his money trying to impress women in the bar. Sadly, Janet was left to pay bills on her own because Sly would spend all of his money in the bar. It was ridiculous! He never had money for more than 2 to 3 days max. Ridiculous! Anyway, the alcohol was a big problem. Being broke was a problem! Ultimately, it is not hard to figure out that domestic violence soon became a huge problem in the household. Research shows that poor education, childhood upbringing, poverty, and economic circumstances are the root causes of domestic violence. Men who feel that they are unable to sufficiently provide for their family due to lack of education, lack of skills, or lack of ambition sometimes resort to controlling their loved ones by violently acting out.

There were nights that Man and his sisters hid behind closed doors, waiting for the abuse to stop. Afterward, they would go to their mother to comfort her. Janet was strong. Her focus remained on her children. As they attempted to console their mother, she reassured them, "Mommy was all right." Her strength was unbelievable. Her resilience was unimaginable. Where was the help? Why didn't anyone put an end to it? How could God allow these things to happen?

According to the National Coalition Against Domestic Violence, "More than 40% of Black women have experienced intimate partner violence (IPV), intimate partner sexual violence, and/or intimate partner stalking in their lifetimes. And more than half of Black adult female homicides are related to intimate partner violence," says the author of the article "*A Layered Look at Domestic Violence in the Black Community.*"

As I write this book, I see that the world is still recovering from the COVID-19 pandemic. Farah Yousry says, "As the pandemic continues to disrupt the lives of millions of Americans, it's also triggering an alarming increase in violence against Black women." It is plain and simple: frustrated men take their frustrations out on the women they claim to love. This has baffled me my entire life. It's weird! To the men out there who think that they can save a battered woman from an unhealthy relationship, stop it. A woman has to make the decision to leave on her own. I have witnessed many times when a woman leaves the abuser only to return sometime later. I have intervened in violent relationships, only to be disappointed by my loved ones returning to the same asshole. Again, I repeat, she has to WANT TO LEAVE. More importantly, she has to know her worth and STAY AWAY! You and your children deserve better!

Man had wished for years that his mother would get away from Sly. He hated Sly.

WEAK MAN (MEN)

Sly's drinking was becoming a major problem in the relationship. When and if he had a job, Sly would spend all of his money within two days of being paid. Janet had to get her from the top. Sly would find a way to avoid paying bills by taking off or leaving work early to get out before Janet returned home from a long, exhausting day at work. Sly never really had a 9-5 job. He worked on houses with Tony. Tony was a white guy who owned plenty of houses. Sly and Tony were opposites, but both were passionate about renovating houses. The difference was that Tony owned the houses. The biggest difference was that Tony was a single father. He was raising his daughter and son alone. Sly spent no time with the family. As a matter of fact, Sly had biological children that he did not spend time with or financially support.

Sly had his own idea of what a man should be. He had grown up in Guyton, Georgia. He was raised by his mother. They called her "Granny." Granny was a strong woman who raised five boys and three girls by herself on the family farm. Granny was known to carry a pistol. She was the reason Sly fell in love with guns at an early age.

Sly dearly loved his mother. He was also a "momma's boy." Just like Man, Sly felt that his mother was the most beautiful woman in the world. On the contrary, Sly treated his women much differently than he would treat his own mother. Granny accepted this from Sly. She never held him accountable for his mistreatment of women or lack of respect for womanhood. Therefore, Sly grew up taking advantage of women and feeling that a woman should be submissive to him.

Granny allowed Sly to believe that respecting her was enough, but respecting and protecting all women is what Granny had failed to instill in her son.

The hate for Sly peaked when Sly decided to take the family back home to his mother's house. All of Sly's brothers and sisters were returning home. Janet and the children were going to the family reunion. It was going to be a great time! Unfortunately, Sly took total advantage of Janet and her children being in an unfamiliar place.

Before leaving for "vacation," Janet had taken the kids shopping for new clothes and sneakers; Janet always made sure that her children were well dressed and clean. She loved dressing up with the children. Janet was a good mom. She made turkey sandwiches and ham sandwiches for the children on the trip. She packed Little Debbie oatmeal creme pies, Oreo cookies, Middleswarth chips, and other snacks for the trip. Janet had a habit of being over-prepared. She was looking forward to having a great time with Sly and his family.

They were traveling to Guyton, Georgia. The road trip was 13 hours from Harrisburg, Pa. They were tailgating with four cars and two vans. Sly was cruising and playing that good ol' down south country music. He was feeling good about himself. Although Janet was the breadwinner, Sly benefitted from all of Janet's hard work. For example, he was driving the vehicle that Janet bought and was living in Janet's new home. From the outside looking in, it appeared that Sly was holding the family down. He was feeling good about himself.

The entourage arrived in the late evening to a crab fest in the backyard. Granny had purchased a few bushels of crabs to welcome everyone. Man was taken aback by his new surroundings because chickens, roosters, and a horse were in the yard. Man was on a farm. He had never believed Sly's stories of raising chickens to eat the eggs. Everyone sat around the bonfire that evening, sharing old stories and eating crabs. That was unusual, too. The crabs were still alive. The teenagers held the love crabs in their hands, chasing the younger kids through the yard. The younger kids loved playing with the claws of dead crabs. Everyone loved seafood. Man decided that he would try to eat crab meat. Aunt Nette had offered the delicacy to him. Toot showed him how to "get to the meat." Man cracked a leg open and ate a little piece. Immediately, his throat started to itch. As always, Man was different from everyone else because he was allergic to seafood. He was unable to enjoy the taste of shrimp and crabs. Everyone knows that Black people love celebrating occasions with shrimp, crabs, and lobsters.

Despite Man being allergic to seafood, Man was able to enjoy some delicious watermelon and pineapples. Man had a sweet tooth, and there were plenty of cakes and pies to eat. Man reminisced and chuckled about having to visit the "outhouse" that night. It was pitch dark. There it stood in the corner of the yard. It was creepy, and spider webs covered the doorway. The door looked as if it was going to fall off. There were a few cinder blocks used as steps to enter the wooden shack. Nervously, Man entered the shack to relieve himself. He was comforted knowing that everyone was outside to protect him.

Sly's family welcomed Janet and the children. That night, Janet sat around with the sister, sipping on moonshine, while the children played in the yard with Sly's nieces and nephews. The next day, Jerry and Nard, the oldest two nephews, took

Man and Toot for a ride in Aunt Mattie's car. Jerry had a girlfriend in Georgia. Her name was Connie. Connie was high yellow with good hair. She had a beautiful smile and a "smokin' hot bangin' body." She had three younger sisters who were just as pretty as she was. Jerry and Nard snuck off with the older sister while Toot and Man sat with the younger sisters on the porch. The girls called the boys "cute." The boys had just received new wallets that Aunt Mattie had made. They proudly displayed their leather wallets to the girls, pointing out the different designs and patterns. Man's wallet had horses running as the pattern. Man really appreciated the gift and felt like he was accepted by Sly's family. Toot and Man laughed and played with the girls until the older boys were ready to leave. That was the last time that Man would see the girls.

The remainder of the day would not be as good for Man. It was horrifying. The only words Man could remember came from his mother screaming, "You gonna bring down here to beat on me in front of my kids and your family?" As Man shares his story, the pain and hurt are evident in his voice, which cracks with emotion.

Sly was on a rampage! His mother, brothers, and sisters idly sat back and watched Sly do the most horrific things to Janet. What had she done to deserve such awful treatment? No one came to her rescue. No one tried to protect the children or shield them from seeing the violence. Sly beats Janet throughout his mother's house. He trapped her in the bedroom and continued his onslaught. Janet's children were the only people who seemed to care. The eldest of the children immediately jumped on Sly. She was throwing "punches and bunches." The two younger siblings followed with more punches to protect their mother. Sly's punk-ass brothers did nothing to stop him. His mother and sisters did nothing. What type of woman does not stand up for other women? What type of mother would allow that to happen in her home? The beating continued until Sly was too drunk and exhausted to keep manhandling Janet.

Sly was the smallest of all the brothers. Man wondered why none of them had put a stop to it. Man thought, "They must be cowards, scared of Sly." Sly's oldest brother was a national champion wrestler. He was a coward. They were all cowards. Man lost respect for all of them on that night. They were not men; they failed to step up as men should to protect all women. How could he respect them? The four brothers could have easily overpowered Sly to take control of the situation. They did nothing. They allowed the brutal beating to take place in front of their mother, their wives, and their children. As the night came upon them, he would see more examples of their unworthiness to be respected as men.

At some point during the day, Janet had been able to call Alfred Cloud—the only man she could depend on. Alfred Cloud drove 13 hours in the middle of the night to pick up Janet and the children. As a drunken Sly slept comfortably in his mother's house, Janet quietly woke up the children and gathered their belongings. No one helped. Not the women. Not the men. No one. Janet and her children had to walk up the dirt road in the wee hours of the morning. Man remembered that the darkness reminded him of a scary movie. It was pitch dark on the road, and there were no streetlights up north. Janet and the children held hands. The children trembled with fear that someone or something would attack them as they escaped the terror. As they scurried to get away, lights shone on them from a vehicle on the road. It was Alfred. He had come to rescue

Janet from the abuse. Again, Alfred was like a brother to Janet; he was her father's favorite nephew.

A few days later, Sly returned from his vacation. Sly was not remorseful, but he was embarrassed that Janet had left him in front of his family. The family pretended as if nothing had happened. Sly apologized, and Janet forgave him. Man hated Sly.

Man remembered the one time when he felt that his mother had responded appropriately to Sly's drunken behavior. As I mentioned before, Sly returned home regularly with a black eye or busted lip after a night in town. One particular night during the summer, Sly had come home drunk and raising hell. Janet and the children had been asleep, but Sly awakened the entire household with his yelling and cursing. Janet was already upset with Sly because it was the beginning of the month, and the bills were due. This was her first major investment—a house.

Sly was supposed to pay the bills first, then go party. However, Sly did not have his priorities in order.

Sly came home that night drunk and caused a disturbance within the house. Janet was sober; she had been awake all night thinking about Sly hanging out and partying with other women. She was furious! Sly had no idea how Janet was feeling when he decided to pick a fight. They argued for a while before Sly agreed he had enough of his woman talking back to him. He was going to shut her mouth. As always, he became physically aggressive by slapping her in the mouth. Without hesitating, Janet threw a straight right jab, punching Sly in the nose. He crumbled. He whined like a little bitch. Janet had busted his nose, and it was bleeding. Man and his sisters happily watched as Sly bled from the nose, but Janet felt bad about hitting him. She quickly came to his aid with a washcloth and towel, helping him to lean his head back to stop the bleeding. Man was confused; he could not understand why Janet was sorrowful about fighting back. Man was disappointed that his mother was caring for this poor excuse for a man. He had started a fight and lost the fight to a woman. Man was happy for his mother to bust Sly's nose, but he was angry that she was submissive to Sly.

Ironically, Man had experienced a similar situation while at school. He was beginning to take notice of girls. He really liked girls! Although the boys in the neighborhood taunted him with claims that he was gay, he was nothing close to being gay. He liked girls! Man had his first unwanted sexual experience at an early age. Man knew what it was like to penetrate a girl. His cousins had taught him. As unreal as it may seem, Man had witnessed and participated in "grown-up things" much earlier than he could physically and mentally understand. So, Man was much more aware of girls' bodies than many of his peers. Some boys were just as "nasty" as Man, and they happened to be his friends. These boys were the reason Man was punched in the nose by Tamika. Yes, a girl punched Man in the nose, too, and his nose was bleeding! Tamika was a pretty, dark-skinned girl who had the figure of a grown woman, even in the third grade. All the boys were fascinated by her curves. While standing in line, waiting to enter the class, the boys had been admiring Tamika from behind. Man stood directly behind her in line. As the boys were sizing her up, Man pretended that he was caressing her butt. One of the boys pushed Man's hand forward, touching Tamika on the butt. Immediately, Tamika turned around and punched Man in the nose. Man did not fight back.

Man was not upset with Tamika but was embarrassed that his nose was bleeding. Man respected Tamika for not allowing a "man" to abuse her. He liked that she was able to protect herself. However, Tamika, like Janet, attempted to console him afterward. Unlike Sly, Man commended Tamika for "taking up for herself." He understood that men should never take advantage of women. Moreover, women have the right to protect themselves from abusive men. Tamika and Man became lifelong friends.

Why do women submit to men? Manon Garcia, the author of *We Are Not Submissive (How Patriarchy Shapes Women's Lives),* has completed a "philosophical exploration of female submission." Is it a woman's nature to be sweet and docile, or have women been taught to portray a role that is convenient for men? A role that prohibits them from having a voice or being able to speak their minds without fear of some form of male retaliation. On the contrary, women are not chastised by only men for being strong. However, other women tend to form unjustified opinions of strong, independent women. For example, how many times have you watched a Lifetime movie that involved a battered woman being convinced to stay with her abusive husband and to be a "good" wife? Too often, the Bible is utilized by men to "help" a woman understand her role in society. In a letter to the Ephesians, Paul says, "Wives submit to your husbands as to the Lord. For the husband is the head of the wife as Christ is the head of the church, his body, of which he is the Saviour."

For anyone who questions the strength of a woman… think about all the women who have survived domestic abuse and are moving on with life, overcoming great obstacles. Do your research. How many women have doctoral degrees compared to men? Women are resilient. They develop a plan and stick to it! Women are powerful! If you have time, check out *The Woman King,* starring Viola Davis. This movie removes any thought of women being passive.

Anyway, although Janet had the ability to leave Sly, she lacked the willpower and confidence to walk away from the dangerous relationship, just like millions of other women. She was attached to her abuser. I believe it's called "Stockholm Syndrome." Wikipedia says, "Stockholm syndrome is a condition in which hostages develop a psychological bond with their captors." Janet was unable to walk away due to mental illness related to the abuse. She was mentally, emotionally, and physically dependent on Sly. Sly's actions would repeatedly put Janet and the children's lives at risk. Without a doubt, he would ensure that they would have nothing if he had his choice. Janet and the children had no idea what was in store for them as the days went by. Man was convinced that Sly was trying to get rid of them. That summer, Sly committed the worst act ever, forcing Man into a role he would continue to play for the rest of his life. He became the savior and protector of the family, including Sly. Despite everything, Man harbored a deep hatred for Sly.

LYRICS FROM TUPAC'S "DEAR MAMA"

When I was sich as a little kid

To keep me happy, there's no limit to the things you did

And all my childhood memories

Are full of all the sweet things you did for me

And even though I act crazy

I gotta thank the Lord that you made me.

There are no words that can express how I feel

You never kept a secret, always stayed real

And I appreciate how you raised me

And all the extra love that you gave me.

I wish I could take the pain away

If you can make it through the night, there's a brighter day

Everything will be alright if you hold on

It's a struggle every day, gotta roll on

And there's no way I can pay you back

But my plan is to show you that I understand

You are appreciated.

Lady, don't you know we love you? (Dear Mama)

Sweet lady, place no one above you (you are appreciated)

Sweet lady, don't you know we love you? (Dear Mama)

Sweet lady

Lady (dear Mama)

Lady, lady!

THE DEVIL'S FIRE

Only a few weeks had passed since the trip to Guyton, Georgia. Janet had forgiven Sly, so he returned to his old ways of drinking until the bar shut down. There were a few times when Man was happy that Sly had gone out partying in the street. Sly was an out-of-control drunk who felt he was invincible. That proved to be far from the truth. Not only had Janet proven that Sly could be bloodied, but others had sent Sly home many nights with a busted lip or a black eye or both. Of course, Janet always responded by providing Sly with ice, heat (when needed), and bandages for his wounds, aches, and pains. The "tough" guy seemed to always get injured in the fight. Man liked seeing Sly's battle scars.

Man was falling in love with the game of football. He felt that it was the one thing that he was able to do to prove his toughness. He took advantage of every opportunity to play at school on the concrete while wearing dress clothes, after school at the playground, on weekends at the "Flat Top," during Harrisburg Cougar football games, and more. Quite often, the neighborhood boys would meet at the firehouse to play. The firemen enjoyed watching the boys play "Freefall!" Freefall is a game of football where every man is for himself. The ball is thrown in the air. And whoever catches the ball attempts to run a touchdown before being tackled. All the boys loved playing "Freefall" because it allowed each of them to display their unique talents. However, most of all, the game allowed the boys to show their toughness. Once the ball was in the air, you had to be aggressive to get it. Then, you had to be either faster or stronger than the others to score. Man was not fast, so he relied on his strength while playing the game. He liked that it always took three or more players to take him down. Man liked that the others respected him while playing the game, and some of them were scared of Man.

The firehouse had become a haven for the boys. There were always "good" men there who talked to the boys about sports and school. The firefighters would help the boys set up bike ramps to perform tricks while jumping off the ramp. Mr. Cooper, who owned a gas station next to the firehouse, would allow the boys to take old tires and plywood to build the ramps. The firefighters were cool! Man trusted the firefighters because they were servants of the community who kept others safe. Remember, Man was lost at five years old, but he remembered the firehouse on 13th Street, which stood as the landmark that he had made it home.

The Firehouse. Home. Man's trust in the firefighters quickly diminished as he placed them in the same category as all the other men who had failed to help. Sly had been out drinking all night. No one knew that he had come home because the family was asleep. As the family slept peacefully, Man awoke to a room filled with smoke. He noticed that the entire upstairs was completely covered in smoke. He went to Janet's room to let her know that the house was on fire. "Ma, the house is on fire!" Janet instructed Man to wake up his sisters and to get everyone out of the house. "Go get Chante and Kieva!" Man followed her instructions. "Ok, ma, I got them!" Next, Janet told Man to run to the firehouse to alert the fire company. It was summertime. Man was wearing nothing more than his "tightie whities"! Nonetheless, Man darted to the firehouse. The firehouse was less than 100 yards away from the house. Seriously, it's less than a football field. As

Man banged on the door, his mother and sisters stood outside watching in disbelief. Man banged on the windows. No one came. The house continued to burn. Man ran back to the house to check on his loved ones and to tell his mother that the firemen did not answer the door. "Go to Aunt Nette's house and tell her to call 9-1-1!" Aunt Nette lived on State Street, about two blocks away. Again, Man raced off in the underwear. He had no shoes on. He was barefoot. He reached Aunt Nette's house within seconds. Thank God, someone answered! To this day, Man does not remember who answered the door. However, he does remember Toot being right by his side. Man told someone to call 9-1-1 and sprinted back to the firehouse. This time, Toot was with him. They yelled, screamed, and banged on the windows and doors until the lights finally came on.

Meanwhile, as Man was running around trying to find help, no one could find Sly. Sly awoke to Janet's and the children's screaming. At that point, he realized what he had done. He had to make it right. Janet and the children had made it out safely, but what about the 80-year-old woman who lived next door? Certainly, he could not have that on his conscience! Sly responded as a Marine should. He quickly sobered up and kicked in the old lady's door! He was able to get her out of her house safely. Doing so, Sly received 2nd and 3rd degree burns on the arms and legs.

The family lost everything! Everything! Sly had come home drunk and decided to make something to eat. As he was heating the grease to fry fish, he had fallen asleep. The children had been taken to Aunt Nette's house to get away from the drama. The adults gathered outside of the house, mesmerized by the devastation. Janet had lost her first home. It was no fault of hers. She and the children had lost everything. They were homeless as a result of Sly's drinking and poor decisions. Sly knew he had fucked up, and he felt guilty about it. As the children sat at his sister's house, Sly cuddled up in a fetal position on Lincoln's playground. He was embarrassed and crying like a baby. Janet's family and friends had arrived, Sly's brothers and sisters were on the scene, and the neighbors were there. Everyone asking the same question: How in the hell did this happen?"

The devil did it!

Sly stayed on Lincoln's playground feeling remorseful for several hours. The Red Cross had arrived at Aunt Nette's house to provide aid to the family. The Red Cross gave the kids Tee shirts, underwear, and hygiene products. As the Red Cross distributed essentials to the family, Man was summoned to Lincoln playground. Sly was requesting Man! Man cannot remember who it was, but he does remember the words they said, "Sly is asking for you, he is crying for you, he won't get up unless you come to get him!" Man was shocked but responded without hesitation. Man walked across the street. He was cool and calm. He understood the seriousness of the situation. From a short distance, he could hear Sly wailing. "Where is my son? I want my son!" He approached Sly, who was still crying and lying on the ground. Man knelt down, hugged Sly, and quietly said, "Let's go." He helped Sly off the ground. He and Sly walked together, hugging each other, and the family followed behind.

Following the fire, Man's feelings for Sly did not change much, but he could tell that Sly had gained a different respect for him. Sly had recognized Man's ability to step up during critical situations. Sly understood that night that if Man had not awoken in time, the family would be dead because of his indiscretions. Despite Sly's sudden admiration for him, man was still angry with Sly. Man felt cheated. He lost the jackets, trophies, and awards he earned while playing football. In his eyes, these were the rewards for "getting tough" or "becoming a man."

The fire changed Man for the worse. He had lost everything. Prior to the fire, he had begun to gain acceptance from his classmates and friends. Now, he was starting from the beginning. He did not have anything: no clothes, no toys, no bed… nothing! Although Aunt Nette offered the family a place to stay, Janet chose to let her daughters live with her sister, Pat. This separation hurt Man because his sisters were his world. When things were bad, it was he and his sisters that comforted each other. Respectfully, they had a song that acknowledged their bond as siblings. "Chante, Kieva, and Maaaaaaan! Chante, Kieva, and Maaaaaan!" That was their song… very simple… their names!

The impact the fire had on Man lasted a lifetime. However, he continued to thrive in the classroom. Man found peace at school. They say schools are to provide a safe and secure environment for students. Man has forever been grateful for the educators who pushed him to be better, no matter the circumstances. If they had known about the disastrous experience, they never offered to help. One thing is for sure, two things for certain: if Man had begun to act out in negative ways, they would have blamed his home environment and parents. Man was taught to "never put the business in the street." Man never said a word to anyone. Man never complained despite losing everything that he had in the fire.

He did not trust anyone. Quietly, he sat in class, sucking his thumb and thinking and always thinking… always.

Working with O.W

O.W. was 6'2" tall, with dark skin with a slim build. He had beady eyes that hid an insincere agenda. This was someone you wouldn't want to see in a dark alley after midnight. O.W. was heavily involved in street life and gangs. He had been sent to juvenile placement for possession of drugs and guns. Immediately, he took ownership of the unit (pod). O.W. intimidated the students and the staff. For weeks, the atmosphere in the pod was tense. O.W. encouraged students to disrespect staff, name-calling, threats of violence, etc. The unit was toxic and chaotic.

One day, during breakfast, O.W. instructed the students to disregard all the rules and staff directives. I intervened. I directed all students to remain calm and return to their eating tables. O.W. outright refused to comply. He decided to challenge me to a fight.

I had the opportunity to converse with O.W. after our negative interaction. I learned so much from this young man. He and I had grown up in the same neighborhood. His father had been murdered in the streets. His mother was in jail. He had young siblings that he was responsible for protecting. He lived from house to house with family and friends. Now, he was locked up in jail, away from his family. While being in placement, he seldom received visitors. He was angry! Rightfully so, he was furious, spitting mad at the world!

I felt terrible that this young man had experienced so much adversity early in his life. We understood each other well. I listened while he spoke of the demons that overtook his childhood. O.W. was wise beyond his years, intelligent, mean, and yet distant - he was me at an early age. I liked his attitude, but I cautioned him that the "attitude" would do him more harm than good. What I noticed was that this young man had a wonderful smile. We spoke at length about how he could improve his life. I shared my concerns with him. Also, I shared my struggles and shortcomings in dealing with my adverse experiences. I pleaded with O.W. to become a better man than me! I told him that he must learn to talk about his problems and deal with life more healthily. I promised to support, mentor, encourage, and help him in any way possible. He needed a MAN in his life.

The Substance Abuse and Mental Health Services Administration (SAMHSA) says that "the impact of childhood traumatic stress can last well beyond childhood." In fact, research shows that child trauma survivors are more likely to have learning problems, including lower grades and more suspensions and expulsions, increased use of health services, including mental health services, and increased involvement with the child welfare and juvenile justice systems.

Reliving the trauma can be psychologically damaging for a child. Although Man appeared to be handling the crisis well, he was constantly reminded of the fire every day. His best friend, Jay Jay, lived on 17th Street. In order for Man to get to his house, he had to walk by the place that had once been his home. When the pain was unbearable, he walked the long way, which added another two blocks. Again, he never told a soul until now.

Man was going into his 3rd season of playing for the Harrisburg Packers. He had made some close friends over the years. They were happy to know that Man was safe and would be rejoining them on the team. Janet was struggling, but she made sure that the children's lives did not change. She did not allow them to dwell in self-pity; she was strong and resilient and wanted her children to be the same way.

Man realized his story would never be told had he not awakened in the wee hours of THAT morning.

Maybe it was time for the house to go… so much evil had been done, as the family would later find out. Sly had committed the ultimate sin! Despite Sly burning the house down, which was unimaginable, Sly had committed the worst sin. No need to discuss it. Figure it out.

FIGHT OR FLIGHT

Living with Aunt Nette was great in the beginning. Unfortunately, no kid likes someone who has interrupted their life; sharing a bedroom and toys is one thing, but now, there is an extra mouth to feed. Someone else that eats big bowls of cereal. No kid is in favor of that. Sooner or later, there will be problems. No matter how strong the relationship is between the children.

Man was in the 4th grade. He does not remember anything good that year. Well, he does recall meeting a young lady, Tammy. She was Man's age, with brown skin and a beautiful smile. Man and Tammy enjoyed listening to Michael Jackson. As they listened to his popular songs, they mimicked his dancing style. On hot summer days, Man and Tammy would sit on the porch, talking about anything and everything. Tammy and Man had something else in common, they both sucked their thumbs. Now that he is older, he wonders what was the reason for Tammy sucking her thumb? Had Tammy been traumatized as a child, too?

Man was finding some peace outside of the home. Man was gaining confidence on the football field. He enjoyed going to practice, never missing practice or a game. Football was a great opportunity to release the pain that he felt from Sly's abuse and neglect. After losing everything, Man felt that enough was enough! He had watched Sly destroy the family home and then cry and whimper as if he were not at fault. He did nothing to replace the things that were lost! Man hated Sly; he was pitiful!

Who could blame Man for the anger he felt? He was a "man" that had lost it all! We all know what happens to someone who feels they have nothing to lose! That person reaches a "point of no return"! Man had reached that point. He was a brave kid who played hard on the football field but a "MAN" who had saved his family. He feared no one. What else was there for him to lose? He had come close to losing his life. Man feared no one!

Some weekends, when the parents had gone out of town, the entire neighborhood stayed overnight. Nard and Jerry were in charge of watching Man and Toot. Stank was old enough to take care of himself. Typically, when Nard and Jerry were in charge, there was a massive sleepover! Everyone from the neighborhood would stay the night: RJ, TJ, Mark, Ronnie, Eddie, Lonnie, Spunk, and whoever's parents allowed them to stay. The boys would have a ball, rent movies from Blockbuster, play video games, have boxing matches, or sit on the porch "Playing the dozens."

Man was the youngest of all the boys in the neighborhood. Everyone was at least two years his elder. There was no wonder why he was the one that was harassed the most. For technical terms, we will refer to it as "bullying." The truth is that because he was the smallest and youngest, he was ridiculed the most. Everyone made jokes at his expense. Again, we can call it "bullying" because mental health professionals, educators, and activists refer to it as such. In the neighborhood, it is considered a "rite of passage." Unfortunately, it can sometimes be taken too far by immature kids.

The weekend sleepovers were enjoyable for everyone. Man was "coming of age". He was nine years old. He liked being around the older boys, especially sitting on the porch until the wee hours, listening to the street stories and jokes.

One weekend, when everyone was staying for the sleepover. Man had fallen asleep before everyone else. Before going to sleep, he had kicked his shoes off. He was wearing his socks. Somehow, while he slept, the older boys had removed his socks. They decided to teach him a lesson. As he quietly slept, he was awakened by the intense heat of a lighter burning his feet! Again, Man was the subject of everyone's laughter. There was absolutely nothing that he could do about it. He looked at his feet, realized they were not burnt, and ensured he never fell asleep before everyone else!

Toot and Man had never had a dispute. Toot did not have to tell Man that he was frustrated with him living at Aunt Nette's house. Toot was the youngest; therefore, he was accustomed to receiving all the attention from his mother and older brothers. Although Man was not related to them, they began to treat Man differently. They joked and played with him. Atari was out! They invited Man to play with them and taught him how to play "*Pac-Man*" and "*Pole Position*." Stank spent more time with Man. Nard and Jerry treated him like their "little brother." Toot and Man's relationship was being tested. Toot had to share his bedroom with Man. Not only that, but Man loved to eat cereal. Now, Toot had to share his Cap N Crunch!

Man did appreciate Sly's brother Alfred. All of the neighborhood boys loved Uncle Alfred. He was the coolest "old head". He kept a nice vehicle with a sophisticated sound system that he would install himself. He was tall, dark, and handsome. More importantly, he had learned to be a gentleman. He was much different than Sly. He always had his children and wife with him. There was never a time that anyone witnessed Uncle Alfred and his wife having a dispute. He had a great personality, always making jokes. Uncle Alfred had a serious side to him, too! He was serious about being a man! He had morals and principles that he instilled in all of the neighborhood boys. "You don't let nobody take advantage of you. Stand up for yourself. I don't care if you win or you lose, but don't let nobody mess with you." He not only preached that to the boys but also showed them how to protect themselves. There were many days when Uncle Alfred would pull up to Aunt Nette's house and get out with two pairs of boxing gloves slung over his shoulder. He helped the boys improve their boxing skills, focusing primarily on throwing the jab. Uncle Alfred also had a unique way of blocking punches. He used his forearms and elbows to block punches. It is very similar to the technique that George Foreman used in his championship fights.

"Keep your chin down," Uncle Alfred would tell the boys as he threw jabs and hooks to help them understand the importance of "tucking your chin." The boys enjoyed being around him. He enjoyed being around the boys. He understood the importance of modeling behaviors for young boys. He was teaching them how to be a man. These lessons would benefit all of the boys as they grew to be teenagers running the streets of Harrisburg.

Toot and Man had a good relationship, but too much time together can put a strain on any relationship. One night, while their parents were out of town, Jerry and Nard had invited everyone to a sleepover. Aunt Nette always left plenty of food for the boys when she was gone. The night would be filled with fun and laughter. The boys would take turns playing

Atari. They mostly enjoyed playing Pac-Man, Ms. Pac-Man, and Pole Position. All the boys had a chance to play, but Toot decided to take Man's turn. He was bullying Man for the position. Man felt that Toot was showing off in front of the other boys. Man stood his ground. He was tired of being treated badly in the presence of the company. Man decided that he was not going to back down. Besides, there were too many people around. He would be called a "punk" forever if he allowed Toot to bully him. Man knew that he was unable to beat up Toot. He knew what the results would be if he made the decision to fight. The other boys cheered them on as he and Toot engaged in their first and only fight. Toot was winning! His punches were faster and sharper than Man's punches. Toot was landing punches to Man's face, but Man kept swinging! Man was relentless! Toot was bigger and stronger, but Man was fighting for his respect. He was fed up with being bullied by everyone. Nard and Jerry stepped in to separate the boys. At that moment, Man punched Toot in the nose. Toot's nose started bleeding. He whimpered, "Y'all held me so he could hit me!" Toot was crying because he had been hit in the nose. He was clearly the winner of the fight. Although Toot had whipped Man's butt, it was a moral and mental victory for Man. He had stopped someone from taking advantage of him. He had proven that he was not a "punk!" Furthermore, he had made Toot's nosebleed. He was no longer scared to fight.

Man began fighting more and more! Most of the fights developed occurred at football practice. The fights were not serious and did not escalate because these were his teammates. Man never held on to the anger because these guys were his friends. However, his attitude changed for the worse; he was horrible. He had grown into a complex person, and he felt that he had to prove himself all the time to prove how tough he was to others. Sly's refusal to accept Man for that innocent and meek child had made him a monster. Sly intended to make him tough, but he created an angry child. Man's innocence had been stolen.

That would not be the only reason for Man becoming a vengeful and mean person. Man loved hanging out with his football buddies. During the summer, they would meet at the pool to have fun. Man and his sisters typically go to Aunt Pat's or PopPops before swimming. During the summer before 5th grade, Man had gone to the pool with his sisters and cousins. While there, he was horseplaying with one of his buddies, Ant McQuay. He and Ant were tight. They had been playing football and going to Ben Franklin for a couple of years. Ant was a running back, and he was fast! He was shifty! Man was bigger than Ant. As the two boys were playing, dunkin' with each other in/out of the water, Pep appeared! He was angry with Man. Man did not even know Pep. He was four or more years older than Man. Man had no idea what was happening. Pep challenged Man to get out of the pool. Pep was already standing on the pool ledge. As Man went to get out of the pool, Pep punched the mess out of him, knocking him back into the pool. Man jumped right back out of the water, throwing punches in bunches! His sister and cousin realized what was happening and quickly joined the fight. Yes, they were swooping Pep! Man was the baby! Pep had crossed the line. Man wanted more. He wanted to fight Pep again!

Again, his innocence and ignorance had been exploited by an older boy. Man was furious. For the first time in his life, he had a black eye!

The world is full of boys who have experienced similar or worse situations in their lives. They are coping with the pain and hurt that traumatized them as a child. Too many of them have been violated by family members or close friends. Man was not special. In the neighborhood, this occurs on a daily basis. Again, the clinicians, health professionals, educators, probation officers, etc., call this bullying. The truth is, that is exactly what happens to boys growing up in impoverished communities. Fighting is a "rite of passage"! At some point, all boys will be challenged to stand up for themselves. FIGHT or FLIGHT! Little Black boys know that the latter is not an option! Not only do men frown on "runners," but women teach their children to fight! Does this sound familiar: "If someone hits you, you BETTER hit them back!" or "If you don't fight back, then I am going to fight you!" Man's mother was no different. Man never told his mother what was happening because he knew what was expected of him. Janet was "raising no sissy." Sly made sure of that, too!

BULL IN THE RING

Football players all over the world know or have played "Bull In the Ring." This is a game that makes aspiring football players quit the game and never return! This game makes warriors tougher, meaner, and downright beasts! The concept of the game is that one player is surrounded by the rest of the team. Each player is given a number. The player in the middle of the ring is "chomping" his feet and "keeping his head on a swivel" (that means quickly moving his head from side to side) and looking for anyone coming to get him! Football players love this game. Players have the opportunity to knock each other to the ground with one hit! Everyone had to stay in the "hitting position." Failure to do so always led to a player getting put on his butt.

The coaches loved the game, too! The coaches would yell and scream, bark and jump around at the sight or sound of a "big hit." Coaches would call the player's numbers. As the number was called, the player would run towards the middle to attack the player. Just one hit. If the player in the middle was knocked down, he had to quickly get to his feet or risk being pummeled again by a different player. The coaches did not let up. They laughed and cheered when players were knocked off of their feet.

Man thirsted to be in the center of the ring. It made him feel unstoppable! He felt like a well-oiled machine, chopping his feet as fast as possible, staying in the hitting position with his head on a swivel. He felt like Lawrence Taylor, Dexter Manley, Wilbur Marshall, and Mike Singletary all in one package. He was a monster linebacker. Yes, there were times in the beginning when Man was knocked to the ground, but it only made him more determined. During those times, Man refused to leave the center of the ring...everyone had to go against him...win or lose! Tears would come streaming down his face, but he was not scared. He was on a mission. Man had been beaten his whole life, and he had decided that would be no more! Win or lose, he would fight until the end. The coaches loved Man for his bad attitude.

There has been extensive research on how trauma fuels success in some athletes. For example, a study led by sports psychology professor Lew Hardy focused on the traumatic experiences of 16 Olympic champions. The gold medalist had been "exposed to trauma as children - including parental death or divorce, physical and verbal abuse or an unstable home environment…" Lew Hardy discovered that athletes like Clara Hughes, Simone Biles, and Andy Murray utilized sports to "escape life at home."

Man had a bad attitude, but he was still a "Mama's Boy"! Man did not like to be hit or yelled at by the coaches. He hated it when the coaches got in his face, yelling, screaming, and, at times, grabbing him by the face mask. Coach Mack was a big guy with huge forearms. Coach Mack would use those big forearms to demonstrate how to attack opponents by "elbowing" them in the head. Players would show up with new arm pads and elbow pads that were purchased by their parents to protect them or make them look the part. Coach Mack would not allow the latter. Looking good, no way. If you were wearing those pads, Coach Mack was going to show you how to "properly" use them. Coach Mack approached the player and asked about the new equipment they were wearing, and then he asked the player to remove the new pads. He would put the pads on himself and TEACH the player the "proper" way to utilize the arm pads and forearm pads.

Football was beginning to develop Man's physicality and emotional and mental state of mind. The team he played for had won 3 Super Bowl championships. Man was full of confidence as a result. His teammates were his friends who lived in the same neighborhood. Players from Uptown, The Hill, and the Southside played together. They became close friends. The relationships among the team members were strong. It was more than just football. These boys were learning about life together.

HIP HOP & THE GANGSTA MENTALITY

Hip-hop began to shape Man's style and personality. The influence of rap music was starting to influence the inner city. Run-DMC was the best group until Dougie Fresh and Slick Rick killed it with "LaDaDi." Run-DMC had all the boys wearing "shell top" Adidas. Dougie and Slick had the whole hood rocking Kangols, gold chains, and a gold tooth. LL Cool J and the Beastie Boys were pumping the suede Pumas. Everyone in the hood thought that they were the best break dancer and "flyest b-boy." Dudes would meet at neighborhood playgrounds to have breakdancing battles and contests. A battle could take place anywhere because, just like in the movies, everyone was walking around with a "Beatbox." The "Beatbox" presented another way for boys to show off their superiority in the hood because everyone wanted to have the biggest and loudest radio. (Watch "Krush Groove" if you need to be reminded of the time!)

Man fell headfirst into the culture, and all of the boys in the neighborhood were heavily influenced by the music, the dance, and the style that hip-hop represented. So much so that while in school at Ben Franklin, the boys would meet in the hallways and staircases to battle each other wearing dress shirts, ties, and hard-bottom shoes. Hip-hop culture had changed the way Blacks talked, walked, and dressed. It was a magnificent time for the Black community.

Although the Black community embraced Hip-hop culture, there were some other things that occurred within the

Black family structure. Black men were unemployed, and they were being incarcerated in large numbers. The War on Drugs and Guns resulted in more drugs and guns on the street than ever before. As a result of a lack of employment, Black men were drinking, smoking, pimping, sniffing coke, and hustling or gambling to make a few dollars. Women were locked up in prisons, too! Women were left alone, working hard to provide for the family and raise the children. Janet was one of many women doing all she could to support her family. Sly was not much help. Emanuel did nothing for the children, nor did he spend time with the children. There were times when Janet would get the children all dressed up to visit Big Momma (Emanuel's mother), hoping that Emanuel would arrive to see the children, but he seldom did. The one time that Emanuel showed up after hours of the children waiting for him, he gave them $5 to split between 3 of them and left. That was the last time that the children would see Emanuel.

Emanuel must have been a hustler. Man knew that his father was a gambler because he remembered his father always playing cards from the beginning of his life. Emanuel had a brother, Johnny, who was a hustler and a gambler, too. They looked like twins. Although they favored each other and enjoyed the same things, Emanuel was much different than Johnny. Emanuel had a bad temper, but he was not confrontational. Johnny, on the other hand, had a big mouth. Rumor had it that Johnny always involved Emanuel in his street-related problems. On the contrary, Emanuel was well respected in the streets, so more often than not, Johnny was given a pass.

Emanuel's love for his brother would cost him his life on a hot summer night in August. Man and his sisters sat in the living room playing games and watching TV. Janet and Sly were upstairs in the bedroom, spending time together. It had been a good day, and there was no arguing or fighting between the couple. The children were joyfully playing with each other. The day seemed to be unusual. However, there was a mysterious calm that lingered in the air.

The sirens could be heard from the ambulance and police racing to the scene. The Speakeasy was located in the alley between 16th & Regina and 16th & Market. Man's family lived on 16th & State Street, about two blocks from Regina Street. The view from the front door allowed the family to witness all the commotion. Within minutes, the phone rang. As Janet went to answer the phone, someone banged on the front door. "Janet, Emanuel got shot! Scottie shot Emanuel!" the person shouted from outside. A crowd gathered at Janet's door to escort her to the scene. The children sat in the living room crying uncontrollably, waiting for their mother to return.

The news spread quickly. Johnny had an argument with Scottie. As always, Johnny called on his brother to fight his battle. Scottie was not a fighter; however, he was a shooter. In the streets, we often hear men say, "I ain't fighting no more. I am shooting!" How often have we heard, "I ain't got time to fight. I'm killin' a nigga!" Scottie had that mentality, too. Emanuel never had a chance. He was gunned down before he could engage in a fight. Scottie had the mindset that many of our young men have today, "I will just kill you, no need to fight." As a result, there are thousands of senseless killings in minority neighborhoods. This has become the norm in our communities. How many young men have been killed in these streets? How many more have to die? When will it stop? By all accounts, Emanuel and Scottie were "friends"! Scottie served less than five years for murdering Emanuel in cold blood.

Emanuel's untimely death reunited the family for a short time. Janet was responsible for handling the funeral arrangements and burial, so she spent a lot of time at Emanuel's mother's home. While Janet was taking care of business, the children were left with Emanuel's family. Man did not like spending time with Emanuel's side of the family. He resented being around them. They had watched Emanuel inflict horrible pain on his mother. Emanuel committed horrific acts in front of his children as his mother and sisters did nothing to stop him. Man hated them as much as he hated Emanuel.

Days before Emanuel's funeral, Man was taken to the barbershop by Emanuel's sister, Aunt Shirley. Man was comfortable going to Mr. Henderson's barbershop. Mr. Henderson was one of Man's favorite people. Mr. Henderson was familiar with Janet's preference for Man's haircut. For some unknown reason, Aunt Shirley directed Mr. Henderson to cut Man's hair like her children's. Aunt Shirley had three sons. She liked for their hair to be cut in a "One." Man's hair was always cut in a "Two" with a Shag. Man was furious! Although his father had been killed, Man could not get past his anger towards Emanuel and his family.

The "haircut" was the "tip of the iceberg" for Man. Man had an odd-shaped head. There was a "knot" that Man never knew was there until the "haircut"! No one else knew that it was there, either! That is, not until the "haircut." Aunt Shirley had made Man the biggest joke on the block. Kids do not understand "death," and they are not sensitive to "death" either. Kids love to joke and play, especially the guys in Man's neighborhood. They can be cruel at times when support is needed. They called Man all kinds of names like "Lumphead," "Rockhead," and "Knothead." Man was totally embarrassed and humiliated; he never told anyone how he was feeling. He became angrier with Emanuel and his family. Emanuel was causing him pain from the grave. Man was furious.

"He passed away, and I didn't cry cuz my anger wouldn't let me feel for a stranger! You say, 'I'm wrong, and I'm heartless, but all along, I was lookin' for a father, he was gone." **(Tupac)**

There were no tears at Emanuel's funeral. Man did not cry. Man tried to force tears out, but he could not cry. There had been too much abuse, too much hurt, too much pain… Man was numb. He was too angry to mourn the loss of his father.

EMANUEL VISITED AFTER DEATH

Emanuel's death was not enough to keep the families together. Man did not see much of his father's family following the funeral. Everyone went their separate way. Johnny never stepped up to be that "missing father figure." Johnny was nowhere to be found. Emanuel came back! Emanuel came back several times! It was clear as day! Some people may think ghosts do not exist, but Man knows that "ghosts" are REAL!

A few days had passed after Emanuel's funeral. Man was hurting badly. He was confused about his feelings toward Emanuel. He knew he was supposed to be sad, but he was angry with everyone, including himself. Why did he not cry at the funeral? Why were his sisters sobbing uncontrollably, but he shed no tears? Janet was devastated by Emanuel's death, but Man, Emanuel's son, felt nothing for his father.

Emanuel's spirit must have been aware of his son's feelings toward him. They say the body is at rest while the spirit lives on, but why would Emanuel appear in the wee hours of the night? What was the reason for the visit? Was there a message to be delivered?

Man was staying overnight at Toot's house. It was one of those weekends when the grownups had gone out of town. Toot's house was built exactly like Man's house because they lived next door to each other. The houses were built with two staircases, one in the living room and another that led from the kitchen to the second-floor hallway. The staircase also provided access to the rear bedroom, which was Toot's. The rear bedroom had three exit doors. A door that led to the balcony, a door that led to the next room, a door that led to the back hallway.

As the boys slept that evening, Man was awakened by a strange presence. He felt like someone was watching him. Toot was asleep. The house was totally dark, which made Man more scared. The door to the hallway was open; the hallway was pitch black, but a figure appeared! It was Emanuel. He was walking in the hallway towards the staircase leading to the kitchen. He called Man's name. The voice was calm and gentle. It seemed as if he was waking Man up from his sleep. Man was terrified. He hid his face under the covers and squeezed his eyes shut. Curious to know if what he saw was an illusion or dream, he uncovered his face and took another peak. Emanuel was still standing there in the hallway. Man shook his head a few times and closed his eyes, only to reopen them to see Emanuel still there. Emanuel looked sharp, as always. He was well-groomed and clean-shaven. He wore a dress shirt and slacks. Despite Man being scared, he welcomed the presence of Emanuel's ghost. He had no choice, no matter how many times he denied the vision, closed his eyes, shook his head… Emanuel was still there.

In the article "Why Do We See Dead People," written by Patricia Pearson, she mentions the concept of "wishful psychosis" in grief. Sigmund Freud was an important figure in describing the "notion of temporary madness featuring willfully conjured visions of the dead." Pearson states, "A person who's lost someone might see the face of their beloved, hear their voice, notice the smell of their pipe or perfume, or simply be struck by a feeling or their presence." In other words, Man may have been traumatized to the point that he was temporarily having psychotic illusions. Man had a mental illness. In 1917, Freud wrote in his essay, *Mourning and Melancholia*, "to encourage people to work towards recovery by severing bonds with the dead: move on and let go, lest sorrow bedevil you and sink you." Emanuel's ghost revealed the impact of adverse childhood experiences that had led up to Emanuel's death. Man was sorry that he had not cried at the funeral. He was disappointed in himself for allowing "the haircut" to anger him, and he regretted that he had never had a relationship with his father. Deep down inside, Man was really hurting. That was the reason for the visit from Emanuel. Perhaps it was closure for the two of them.

The death of Emanuel devastated Man, but he kept himself together by going to school, getting involved in activities, and sucking his thumb. Emanuel's death had occurred a few weeks before Man entered the fifth grade. Man recalled that there was only one teacher who mentioned the death of his father. He was Mr. McGarrity, and he was Man's favorite teacher. The teacher did not make a scene. He walked up to Man quietly and said, "Hello, I am sorry to hear about your father." He did not offer a hug or a quiet place to hang out when Man was overwhelmed with grief. The expectation was for Man to deal with his loss without having a behavioral problem. The biggest complaint that the teachers discussed with Janet was that Man was too old to be sucking his thumb. No one thought that he had been traumatized to the extent that he found comfort in sucking his thumb. Not only was it a coping mechanism, but "thumbsucking" prevented Man from telling the family's business. Consequently, the football field was not the only place where Man was brutal and aggressive.

Man developed a mindset after his father died. They shared the same name, Emanuel. Man vowed never to let anyone do to him what had been done to his father. Man was going to prove to everyone that he was tougher than his father. He was out to make a new name for himself.

THE BOSS PACKER

The Crossroads article *"Understanding How Men Grieve"* describes grief as a "unique experience." What that means is that individuals will cope with grief in different ways that help them through difficult times. The article says, "When we think of grieving, most of us consider sadness and crying to be typical. But there are many symptoms of grief. For men used to hiding tears, other symptoms include withdrawal, irritability, anger, thoughts of death, and substance abuse." For younger children, they grieve differently than adults. Rachel Ehmke states in the article *"Helping Children Deal With Grief"* that it is normal for a child to be "depressed, guilty, anxious, or angry" at a person, anyone, and/or anything. Man was angry with everyone.

Man entered his fifth-grade year with a chip on his shoulder. No one seemed to notice the changes in him. He continued to exceed the expectations in the classroom despite his father being killed weeks prior to school beginning. The only concern was that he was too old to be sucking his thumb. Without saying it, the teachers probably thought that he was too big to be sucking his thumb. Thinking back on it, Man still wonders why no one made a connection to the traumatic experiences that had occurred in his life. Man was silently calling out for help. He began to feel alone and angry. Although he had friends at school, his neighborhood buddies attended different schools. As a result, Man sucked his thumb, kept his thoughts to himself, and focused on his academics while at school. The teachers never thought about trauma-informed care or empathy as long as Man behaved and met the academic expectations.

For the most part, Man was able to control himself in the presence of adults. He knew how to deceive the grownups; just stay quiet and do your work. There were a few times when Man's anger earned him a disciplinary referral at school. Every scuffle that Man was involved in at school was with one kid. This kid was the biggest student in the school. The guy was taller than most students and weighed about 250 lbs. He was an intelligent, big guy, too! For some reason, he and Man could not get along together. It was weird. At times, they were friends, but there was this rivalry between the two of them. Man always felt that he was being bullied by the bigger kid. Man, vowing never to let anyone hurt or kill him after his father's death, being consumed with anger, had several fights with the big guy that year. The fights were short and quick. No one ever got hurt. Man was much smaller. He weighed about 100 lbs. He liked fighting the bigger boy. He was faster than the big guy. Surprisingly, the fights always led to wrestling! Man never lost. He held his ground with the bully. On the contrary, Man had never fought in school until that year. He was angry, lost, and alone.

After Emanuel's death, Man felt that he was responsible for the safety and security of himself, his mother and sisters, and anyone that he considered a friend. There was this kid, Norm, who was from Trinidad, who had moved into the neighborhood. This kid was tough; he looked like a killer. He was short and muscular. He had a bald head and was cock-eyed. Most of the kids in the neighborhood feared him because he had a name for fighting. Norm was scary-looking and had a "mean stroll" like all the "hard rocks."

One day, as Man and his football buddies stood at the bus stop, Norm decided to do his thing. Norm started to bully Man's friends for no reason. It all began because Norman wanted to sit on the swing, so he decided to make someone get off. Man had been bullied by the older boys in the neighborhood, but now, he was witnessing Norm bullying a younger kid from the neighborhood. Man hated bullies because they took advantage of weaker and smaller kids who were afraid to stand up for themselves. Man watched as the younger boy reluctantly gave up his swing. Although the younger boy had family members with him, no one dared to address what was happening. Man became infuriated. These were his teammates and friends that he played with every day. Man had always been intimidated by Norm, but without any hesitation, he politely told Norm to leave them alone. Norm was shocked; he could not believe Man was "talking tough"! After all, Man went to Ben Franklin and wore dress clothes – a pair of "Baggies," Playboy shoes, a shirt, and a tie.

Norm had a devilish laugh; he was a very confident guy. He asked, "What are you gonna do about it?" Football has made Man more confident year after year. He had learned to face his fears despite being terrified most of the time. Man responded, "It's whatever." Norm asked Man for a "fair one"! Man had not been in many fights, but Peppy had started something when he stole Man at Jackson Lick. Man had spent many days standing in front of the mirror, boxing his own reflection. He was throwing jabs, hooks, bobbin and weavin', vicious uppercuts, and keeping his eyes open. Man was not going to be caught off guard again. He kept his eyes on Norm as he dropped his book bag to prepare to fight.

Man and Norm faced off, posturing to fight by the fence on the outside of the playground. The crowd, boys and girls from Lincoln, Woodward, and Ben Franklin, encircled the boys to watch them "throwdown." Norm had a sinister grin on his face and stared at Man in his eyes. Man's fear and uncertainty were hidden as he threw the first punch that landed on the right shoulder. Norm laughed. Both boys went in… throwing punches in bunches! Man's hands seemed to be faster, and his punches sounded harder as they connected with Norm's face and head. Man was throwing punches with "mean intentions!" Norm must have felt he could win with a "jack slam!" He was known for "taking dudes on a ride to see the devil." Norm was short and stocky, so he lowered his level and scooped Man up! The crowd was going crazy! Man kept his cool as Norm lifted him off his feet. Man was left-handed. He was so conscious throughout the fight as if he could see everything around him. While in the air, he realized the fence was within arm's reach. He grabbed the fence with his right hand and proceeded to "drop bombs" on Norman's head! Norm could not withstand the punches to his brain. He became weak and weary and could no longer hold on to Man. The crowd cheered Man on. Mari, Kev, and Corry knew Man had their back forever! Man had won one for the hood and gained the respect of his peers.

Reflecting on the time, Man believes he had no choice but to come to his friend's defense. There was no one else to defend him or them! Many of the guys from the neighborhood were being locked up in Woodside, VisionQuest, and Glen Mills for stealing cars. Man was afraid to steal cars, and he did not know how to drive and neither wanted to. The fellas made it sound and look so easy, "Got a dent puller and screwdriver, we out!" Wayne, TJ, Michael, and neighborhood buddies were being locked up at an early age. Simple, yeah, but the price for joyriding was a cost that Man was unwilling to pay. There were a few times when he "jumped in" for a ride to school, but for the most part, Man avoided the stolen cars.

Decision-making is key to our survival! It is those times when everyone is doing it, and you feel like a "Cornball" for doing the "right thing." Well, you better think and rethink the situation over and over again to determine if you are willing to lose your freedom or your life trying to be like everyone else. Learn to practice INTELLIGENCE OVER EMOTIONS!

One of the questions on the ACE test is, "Was a loved one incarcerated during your childhood?" Many of Man's closest friends went to "juvy" in elementary and junior high school. For a young man growing up without a father or any brothers, that has a devastating impact on your daily life. At times, you would rather be locked up with them rather than alone on the streets.

In hindsight, Man was confused! Man was desperate to prove himself. Man was angry as hell! He was ready for "whatever" the streets had to offer him. As a matter of fact, he welcomed the drama.

A few weeks later, Hamilton School caught on fire. Hamilton was a much different school than Benjamin Franklin. The project kids and uptown kids went to Hamilton School, which was considered to be one of the toughest schools in the city. The kids at Hamilton were able to wear whatever they chose to wear to school… T-shirts, sweatsuits, jeans, sneakers… whatever they wanted to wear. The difference was barely noticeable among the elementary girls; however, the stylish outfits and trendy sneakers the Hamilton boys wore distinguished them from the preppy Ben Franklin boys. The union of the two schools created a hostile environment. As we know, males are territorial. For young boys growing up in the city, protecting their neighborhood was a top priority. Better yet, in the "hood," protecting your manhood was the #1 priority.

The students were not alone when it came to tolerating the presence of the new, unruly students. The teachers were forced to share their space and deal with disorderly, disrespectful students who were not accustomed to the "high expectations" of the "prestigious" school. At Benjamin Franklin, there were procedures for all activities, classes, and programs. Hamilton students often disrupted their daily routines and ignored the procedures. One day, while waiting for the bus to go home, a boy from Hamilton began to tease Man. Man had seen the boy in school many times; his name was Jesse. He was a cool guy; he had a "hard stroll," wore a gold chain, and had both of his ears pierced. He was in the fifth grade, too! The girls appeared to adore him. He was cool!

Jesse was taking advantage of the situation because he was with his friends. He kept calling Man a "punk." Again, Man was dressed in "baggies," Playboy shoes, a shirt, and a tie. Initially, Man kept his cool, practicing INTELLIGENCE over EMOTION. Thinking about the disadvantage of being alone, Man knew that he would get "rushed" if he played into Jesse's antics. Nonetheless, Man was so angry that smoke was probably coming out of his nose. Man withstood the torment for a few seconds, which seemed like hours, before being reassured by his Benjamin Franklin friends that he was not alone. At that point, Man unleashed his anger on Jesse in front of Ben Franklin and Hamilton school students.

Man was able to keep it together on the football field. He was forced to be respectful and behave himself at practice and during the games. The coaches' expectations never changed despite the trauma that Man was dealing with at home. On the football field, Man attempted to fight many times, but the coaches discouraged this behavior. The coaches preached that the team was a family. Whenever there was a disagreement amongst the boys, the coaches would bring the entire team together to address the issue in a more relevant way than fighting. The coaches used unhealthy behavior to improve the boys' football skills. Coach Chis was the head of the household, but every coach took on the role of being a father for the boys. The coaches had high expectations for the players on and off the football field.

The bond that was formed in those early years would last a lifetime for the players, cheerleaders, parents, and coaches!

That is the reason this book is dedicated to the Harrisburg Packers Coaches, Team Moms, Players, Cheerleaders, and anyone affiliated with the Harrisburg Packers Organization.

The most beloved Coach Charles Chisolm, Skip House, Vernon Lipscomb, Sheman Cunningham, Sean Broden, Jimmy Mathis, Nate McWhite, Dwight Henry, Coach White, Perry Landon, Steve Holmes, Roger Dixon, Will Marshall, Shawn Gillespie, Troy Bullock, Barry Rector, Bryant Stafford, and all those men who gave their time and efforts to improve the lives of young boys in Harrisburg.

This book has not been written based on extensive knowledge, data, and/or research. Scrutinize this book as you will. However, I must say that this is to inform you of all the challenges and struggles that children face on a daily basis.

Not all children respond the same to trauma, so look for signs and ask questions. You may ask, "What makes you an expert on adverse childhood experiences?" My response is that I do not consider myself to be an expert or an authority on mental health or adverse childhood experiences. Unfortunately, I have experienced more adverse and traumatic childhood experiences that continue to haunt me and influence the way that I interact with others. I beg you to consciously focus on three things for your child's ultimate success...EDUCATION, ENVIRONMENT, and EXPOSURE! I call these the "3 BIG E's"! But wait, there is a fourth Big E... EXPECTATIONS for your children must be kept high and you must do all that you can to HELP your children reach and exceed the expectations.

MESSAGE TO WOMEN

Ladies, you are the strongest beings on earth! You must know your self-worth! Recognize the strength that you have from within! You must understand that if a man is beating you, if he is mistreating you, then it is time to go! "Yes, you should give your partner an opportunity to change, but set a time limit. Have a plan so that you have an idea of whether they continue with the same behavior! We all struggle; this is true, but our struggles should not affect the lives of others." Therefore, ladies, if he has problems. Please empathize with him, but do not place you and/or your children in a dangerous situation. Love him, but love him from a distance.

Next, ladies, you must understand that your children do not and will not forget. You may think that your child is at the age where they will forget what happened as they grow older. That is far from the truth! The fact is that your child will remember, the same way that Man has been able to walk you through the days of his life, your children will one day recount the days of their lives. However, there may be some foggy areas and the trauma that your child encounters will impact them for the remainder of their lives. Therefore, it is imperative that you find the strength to leave. You cannot tell your children how much you love them and continue to jeopardize their well-being. Your children will remember that you loved the abuser more than you loved them.

Ladies, if you choose to stay in an unhealthy relationship, give your children the opportunity to succeed. Whatever it takes to get them away from the situation, please do so immediately. How does that happen? Well, you must get your children involved in something positive: the Boys and Girls Club, Big Brother/Big Sister, Girl Scouts, youth sports, faith-based organizations, etc. You should support your child in whatever it is he/she is interested in. Get them away from the situation!

The other thing that you must do is allow those positive men in these organizations to work with your son effectively. The men who take time to invest in your child are sincere. Yes, I understand that you must protect your child from dangerous men, but let's be honest, you can't defend yourself from a dangerous man! Your loves and insecurities cause you to make poor decisions that inadvertently destroy your children's lives. These men in the community are the only hope that you have. These guys are here to do nothing more than shower your child with love and affection. Yes, they have rules and expectations! That is what "good" men do! "Good" men have high morals and values, so they instil them within your child. Something that they may be missing at home. So, ladies, back up, get out of the way, and let these "good" men do their job!

You make it very difficult when you question everything that is going on. Oh, your child got yelled at. And? They probably needed to be yelled at! Oh, your child got snatched up. So! They probably needed to be snatched up! Stop trying to protect your child under the wrong circumstances! That is bullcrap! Do not over-protect your children from the ones that hold them accountable. Following the rules and being respectful will serve your child well in the future.

Do not put your children on meds! If they need them, fine, but try your hardest to avoid placing your child on meds! Do you not know that this labels them as mentally ill? Has your child been diagnosed with ADD, ADHD, Bi-polar, ED,

Asperger, Autism, or anything else—STOP TELLING THEM OVER AND OVER AGAIN—" You have this…." or "It's because of this…" You are killing your child's motivation and hope. Stop making excuses for them! Then, they will stop making excuses for themselves.

By the way, ladies, if you tell your son to hit girls back when he is hit, then you are doing nothing more than creating a future "woman beater!" I've lost count of the number of phone calls I've made to mothers who justify their sons hitting girls. The typical follow-up questions are: "Well, what did she do to him?" or "Did she hit him first?' My thought has always been: What kind of nonsense is that? Does it matter what she did to him? Why is it ever okay for a boy to hit a girl?" I understand that there are circumstances in which one must protect oneself. However, I truly believe that most men are strong enough to grab and hold the woman until she calms down or until help arrives. Furthermore, men's awareness should be heightened the very first time that a woman becomes aggressive. Fight or flight! Well, if you are a wise man, then you know that the former will have you behind bars. Run! Run! Run! The only option that you have is to separate yourself at all costs.

It goes back to that old saying: Children learn what they are taught! This means "if mommy said it is okay to hit girls, then it is okay to hit a woman, especially if she has hit you first." When he is arrested as an adult for domestic violence, you must understand that you created that monster. Teach your boys better! Teach them to treat all women with respect! Teach them to honor women! Teach them to protect women! Teach them to walk away! I heard it said, "A man treats his woman the same way he treats his mother." Think about it.

Again, ladies, it all begins with you discovering your true worth. It would help if you stopped settling for any and everything. You might have to reconsider the type of man that attracts you. You might have to change some things about yourself. Regardless of it all, treat yourself like a queen. In order for someone to treat you like a queen, you must treat yourself like a queen first!

Respect to all the ladies who never subjected themselves to domestic violence. Respect to all of the SURVIVORS of domestic violence. Respect to all the ladies who walked away. Respect to all of the ladies who fought back. Respect to all the ladies who know their worth!

MESSAGE TO THE MEN

Men, we have failed our children, our families, and our communities!

First of all, shame on you if you are a "woman beater"! You must be better than what you may have witnessed as a child. Break the cycle! If you were someone who witnessed a man beat their loved one, how could you become that? You cannot use excuses such as "That's all I know" or "My dad did it." There is no way possible that you could think that was excusable. As we go out into this world, we learn the difference between right and wrong. Once we know, we make a decision to do good or do bad, to do right or to do wrong. We can rid our families of generational curses that haunted our ancestors and our living loved ones. So many secrets, too much trauma– we must be different from those who came before us. As they say, "When you KNOW better, you DO better!"

If you are a dude that watched a woman get slapped around or beat down, well, F&#K YOU TOO! You are just as bad as he is! There is nothing that she could have done that he could not walk away from. It is very simple: if she is doing something that you do not like or agree with, get rid of her! Again, I understand that everyone has problems, but if the problems upset you to the point of physical violence, then it is time to walk away. Let them figure it out on their own.

Fellas, our job is to protect women, all women! Let's do our job!

Next, if you think the children will forget the pain and heartache, you are wrong. Your number one priority is to keep your family safe. Your children will never feel safe around you or anyone else. They will lose all trust in adults. Some of you may think that this is only true if you have physically harmed your child, but mentally and emotionally, the child will be scarred for life. If you have sat back and allowed domestic violence to take place in front of children, they will remember you, too! You will be labeled as the "coward" who did nothing. Maybe this is not always true, but if children feel the way that Man felt… sheesh… someone better do something!

I have to talk to all of the men who feel that it is okay to touch little girls. That is some filthy shit! Why in the world would a man have to violate a little girl when there are plenty of beautiful, established women out here looking for a man? The shit is disgusting! It does not matter if she is two years old or 15 years old! There are lots of gorgeous women who are desperate for a man. Ladies, please know that I do not intend to demean you. I am simply saying there is never a reason for a man to involve himself with a child. Some so many men have been "let off the hook."

Do you know how many fathers, grandfathers, uncles, cousins, brothers, stepdads, and all types of men have been given a pass? Millions of men have avoided prison because of the "great family secret"! The "Great family secret" is that everyone in the family is aware of the pervert in the family. The pervert violated someone in the family. Everyone in the family knew of it! No one in the family told the "great family secret." He got away with it. Chances are that he violated more than one person in the family. However, because we are too prideful, we allow the perpetrator to get away with it to avoid family embarrassment. This is shameful! We sacrifice the goodness of our children because we do not want others to judge us. Therefore, we live by the old saying: "Don't be puttin' family business out in the streets!" This is the "Great family secret!"

The long-term effects of allowing you men to get away with these crimes have ruined generations of children. As a counselor, I have noticed an increase in childhood molestation. In particular, I have seen a spike in the number of children who are violating their younger siblings. Too often, the perpetrators have been violated by a loved one. These young molesters are doing to others what was done to them. Remember, "Children learn what they are taught." Victims become perpetrators. We must stop allowing these predators to get away with hurting our children. If we truly want to protect them—all of them – then we must do what is right. We must end the generational trauma.

Working with Kaylan

Two students disrupted class. The principal and I arrived at the classroom as the students were having a verbal altercation, which escalated into a physical fight. We separated the girls; the principal escorted his student in one direction, and I guided the other (Kaylan) in the opposite direction. To ensure that the situation did not escalate to a more severe problem, the principal requested that I keep the young lady with me in my classroom for the remainder of the day.

I believe that young girls desperately need a positive father figure in their lives. At the time, I was raising my daughter as a single father. Kaylan appeared to need a positive male role model, too! She sat in my classroom without causing any problems. She participated in the lesson. Throughout my instruction, I would walk to the rear of the school to check on her. I noticed that there were scars on her forearms, scratches, and welts like those on an enslaved person. I had seen this many times while working in a juvenile facility. I had seen young ladies use their fingernails, writing utensils, erasers, staples, and almost anything available to scratch their arms as a coping mechanism. Quietly and discreetly, I told Kaylan, "I need to talk to you." Although this was my first introduction to Kaylan, she knew I was not a threat and was genuine in my efforts to protect her. Every time I walked to the rear of the class, I jokingly said, "Yes, ma'am! We are gonna talk!" Finally, she asked, "What do you wanna talk about?" Discreetly, I pointed to the scars on her arm. Surprisingly, she did not become defensive; she was open to a conversation. She responded, "So, when do you want to talk?" My response was, "ASAP!"

After school, Kaylan had to pick up her younger siblings from school. Kaylan's mother worked two jobs, so Kaylan cared for the young ones. Kaylan promised that she would return the following day to finish the conversation. Kaylan kept her promise. Kaylan shared with me that she had been the victim of sexual abuse. She had told her mother, but her mother did not believe her. She felt helpless. Kayla was coping with the abuse by self-harming. She was confident in saying, "I am not trying to kill myself, but it feels good; it calms me down."

I have heard this many times from self-harming individuals. I ask, "How do you know when it has gone too far?" What healthy habits or activities can you do to get the same feeling? What can I do to help?" During these times, being judgmental will cause the student to withdraw. So, I was cautious. I was there to listen, not to talk.

As I write this story, I am forced to reflect on my own shortcomings as a man. I have stated many times that a man is expected to protect his loved ones. Man held a deep resentment for all the men who failed to intervene in the violence against his mother. Man held on to that anger for years. While reflecting on my relationships with my nephews, I am saddened by the thought that I failed to protect them. My oldest nephew does not like me. He has every right to feel this way because he believes that I did not protect him as a child. I would never allow anything to happen to him. Truthfully, I had attempted to whip the assailant many times, but others thought that I was just being "mean." He had even threatened to stab me, but I was seen as the aggressor. The day came years later when my nephew was ten years old. The perpetrator had grabbed my nephew by the cheeks, leaving bruises on both sides. He had hit my nephew. I had vowed my entire life to protect my loved babies. I searched high and low for this guy… bars, stores, uptown, downtown, everywhere until I was told of his exact location. Coincidentally, as I was about a block away from the spot, I could see a Mercedes parked in the middle of the street. I recognized this as my father's car. From a distance, I could see two men about to engage in a fight. The bigger guy was aggressively approaching the smaller guy. Immediately, I put my car in the parking position. I jumped out of my car and sprinted the entire block.

Let's just say that I whooped his ass really bad. Nonetheless, that did not reassure my nephew that I would protect him. There was too much damage done that I did not know about. There were too many secrets! Regardless, he relied on me to keep him safe, and in his eyes, I failed! He once said, "If anyone should have known what was happening, his uncle should have…" His uncle was his hero who did not rescue him at the right time!

Gentlemen, please understand that we have a huge responsibility as MEN to protect our loved ones, our children, and our families! Do not question how you do that. Just do it! It is like homie said in *Hustle and Flow* ...

"I am always right when I am right, I am right when I am wrong, I could have been right, and I am right because I could have been wrong!" 50 Cent responded with, "That makes sense." The truth is that we should always go with our gut. My gut told me to deal with the person who harmed my nephew years before I physically put my hands on him. The damage was done. There is no right or wrong way to BE A MAN… just knocks the lights out!

MEANINGFUL INTERACTION WITH MEANINGFUL INTENTIONS

Men must have an outcome in mind when working with our young children, specifically boys. Boys tend to be very impressionable in the early stages of their lives. They copy what they see in others, whether males or females. Often, we hear and talk about in small circles how certain men have "female qualities." Now, some of these young boys may be dealing with sexual identity issues. Others mimic what they see around them. Therefore, men, we must have "meaningful interactions with meaningful intentions" when teaching, coaching, and mentoring our boys! Everything that we do must have a desired outcome. We have to model the behaviors that we expect from our children.

What is meaningful interaction? What are meaningful interactions?

"Borrowed Fathers"

Borrowed Fathers are men who give their time, love, affection, support, experience, wisdom, money, transportation, and everything that a man should give to a child that he wants to be successful. Unfortunately, these men are not the paternal fathers of these children, but they take on the responsibility of raising our children. In short, borrowed fathers take on the role of being a "father" to many of the children in the community. Borrowed Fathers make a difference in our community. Borrowed Fathers save lives!

Thank you to all the "Borrowed Fathers" in our community! Thank you to all the "Borrowed Fathers" that saved Man's life.

Talk to Your Children

Working with a special needs student

A few years ago, I was in class working with students with special needs. As class began, a young lady arrived late. Immediately, I noticed that the young lady appeared to be crying. The young lady walked to her seat and sat down. The teacher, who opened the door for the student, paid no attention to the student. She had not remembered which student had entered the class. The teacher returned to her desk; she said, "Oh, who was that who just came in? Oh, there you are." The young lady could not compose herself and approached the teacher's desk to confide in her. She tells the teacher that a stranger attempted to abduct her on the way to school. The response from the teacher was a 5-second hug, and the student was sent to her seat.

I could not believe what I had witnessed at the time. I truly felt that the young lady deserved more. As educators, our priority is the safety and security of our students. The teacher continued with the daily lesson, neglecting the needs of the students. Where was the empathy? What was the teacher's priority? The young lady had been traumatized! How could she learn under those circumstances?

The young lady sat traumatized by the threat of abduction. A paraprofessional and I decided to remove the student from class and ask more questions. Where did it happen? What did the perpetrator look like? What kind of vehicle? What color was the car?

We notified the police and her parents. A counselor was available for the young lady. She went on to have a good day.

Our role as caregivers is essential for effectively educating our students. Trauma-informed care requires professionals to empathize with students while providing a safe space. Trauma-informed care equips teachers with the tools to interact with students suffering from adverse childhood experiences effectively.

There are many proven ways to get to know your children. Quality time is the best way! However, the time spent with your children should be meaningful. How can you capitalize on the time spent with your children? It is a simple answer: ask questions that build on the conversations. You do not have to seek professional help or rely on clinical techniques to improve your relationship with your children. Mental health professionals refer to it as "motivational interviewing." Reporters refer to it as 5W1H. English teachers use it to help students identify parts of speech and short story elements. Nonetheless, the goal is to discover information. Talk to your children! More importantly, listen to your children!

PURPOSE

In the end, this book has been written for three purposes. If you have read this book in its entirety and concluded that it was written to express the hate that Man had for Sly, you are very wrong. As you will discover later, Man loved Sly as if he were his biological father. Therefore, the purpose of this book is not to tear Sly down or expose him as a bad person. That would be a waste of time and far from the truth. And if you think Man disliked the older boys. Wrong again. The love that the neighborhood boys had for one another has grown into a lifetime friendship. The boys are still inseparable, linked for a lifetime.

The main purpose of the book is to write and release the hurt and pain that Man carried with him through life. Hence, Man shared his story with the world so that others would not be ashamed to share their stories with others. Some so many people are carrying around baggage from the past, the burdens that weigh them down and prevent them from reaching their full potential. Man is no different than all the little boys growing up in the ghetto. Honestly, Man is every man! Young boys growing up in the city, the suburbs, and the country can relate to the stories shared in this book. Boys and girls all over the world are experiencing childhood trauma, and no one seems to understand how it affects their emotional and mental growth. Man understands how it feels to go unnoticed by teachers, principals, and counselors. Man understands that when you tell your story, the adults will discredit you or blame you for the situation. However, Man also understands that carrying those burdens through life does you more harm than good. Your trials and tribulations will continue to beat you down until you are either depressed, strung out on drugs, locked up, or dead. Let it go! Talk to someone! Write and Release! That is the main purpose of this book.

That does not only pertain to boys! Man wants the girls and women to Write and Release too! Let it go! Your story is important! Talk about whatever it is that is holding you back! Let it go!

Write and Release.

READ IT!

RELATE TO IT!

WRITE ABOUT IT!

RELEASE IT!

Man's journey was not easy, but it was necessary. In sharing his pain, he discovered strength and resilience he never knew he had. By opening up about his past, he found healing and a sense of purpose. His story is a testament to the power of vulnerability and the importance of speaking out.

Did she know that the mental and psychological abuse would negatively affect the children for the rest of their lives? Perhaps not. But this book aims to shed light on these unseen scars and to offer hope to those who bear them.

How does developing strong relationships help heal the effects of trauma? Through connection, we find validation and support. Strong relationships provide a safe space to express our deepest fears and pains. They remind us that we are not alone in our struggles and that healing is possible.

As you close this book, remember that you have the power to write your own story. You have the strength to overcome your past and to shape your future. Take Man's message to heart: Write and Release. Let your story be heard. Let your voice be a beacon of hope for others.

REFERENCES

1.   Bonzcar, Thomas Prevalence of Imprisonment in the U.S. Population, 1974-2001., U.S. Department of Justice, August 2003.

2.   Coburn Place. "A Layered Look at Domestic Violence in the Black Community". 2023 Coburn Place.

3.   https://athletesforhope.org/2019/10/kids-trauma-and-sports-how-athletes-can-make-a-difference

4.   https://theconversation.com/the-surprising-role-of-childhood-trauma-in-athletic-success

Made in the USA
Columbia, SC
03 September 2024

edd0d1dd-ec18-424d-88d6-41437d73c78dR01